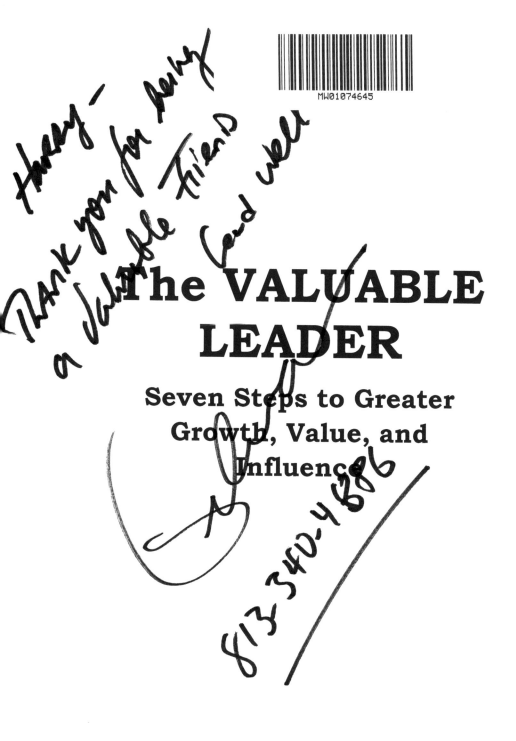

The VALUABLE LEADER

Seven Steps to Greater Growth, Value, and Influence

Harry —

Thank you for being a valuable friend

...and well

813-340-4886

The VALUABLE LEADER

Seven Steps to Greater Growth, Value, and Influence

Velma Knowles

Praise for *THE VALUABLE LEADER*

"In business, leadership is everything and *The Valuable Leader* is everything you need to know! Theory coupled with memorable stories makes this a 'must read' for every person in a leadership position."

Colleen Sweeney, RN, BS, CSP Founder of Sweeney Healthcare Enterprises

"Anyone who knows Velma Knowles recognizes that she avoids complexity and worn-out jargon. She writes like she speaks – with sincerity, emotion and straight-up candor. The stories she shares to support her seven steps to being a Valuable Leader offer valuable lessons and insights to inspire those around you."

Ruby Newell-Legner, CSP, Fan Experience Expert and Founder of 7 Star Service

"Whether you are a teacher, parent, leader of a church fellowship group, the manager of a department or the CEO of a company, this book is an indispensable resource for how to be a better and more enlightened and valuable person tomorrow than you were today."

Dr. Vickie H. Williams, Director of Elementary Curriculum and Professional Learning

"As a professional leadership speaker I have read countless books on leadership. In this book Velma outlines a great formula to achieve greater growth, value, and influence. It would be a great addition to your leadership library."

Chris Robinson, Faculty Member, The John Maxwell Team.

"Regardless of your leadership style, *The Valuable Leader* provides the reader with a fundamental framework of best practices to ensure success to any individual leading a group. Velma emphasizes key leadership skills such as; active listening, showcasing the benefits of working as a team and how to effectively collaborate ideas and brainstorm. This book reminds leaders that every employee brings value to their organization and should be treated as such. Velma Knowles gives us some of her real life experiences and pulls in great minds like Stephen Covey in order to create what appears to be a B.I.B.L.E (basic instructions before leading everyone) for new leaders and existing leaders alike. Do not get caught without this book."

Verlyn Forde-Drummond, National Recruitment Manager

"If you aspire to become an outstanding leader, this book is a must read. *The Valuable Leader* is a practical guide for nurturing the seven specific qualities all leaders need to be successful."

Randy Keirn, District Chief, Lealman Fire District

True leadership requires the courage to grow intentionally and continuously so that we can make a greater positive impact in the lives of others. Through personal experiences and shared stories, *The Valuable Leader* encourages us to take another look at where we are as leaders and to thoughtfully consider how we can become more effective in serving others.

Kuthy Kasten, Founder, CEO – Lion Crest Leadership

"Velma presented *The Valuable Leader* in an easy to understand and applicable style. She utilized her own life-experiences as real examples for the ideas. If you are looking for an applicable and actionable leadership book, *The Valuable Leader* is a must read."

Dan Gunadi, Information Technology Leader

"Emerging and seasoned leaders can both benefit by reading what Velma has written about how to become a Valuable Leader in both business and life. Her seven steps are concise, and easy to understand. She knows what it takes to be a leader who adds value."

Heather Kasten, President & CEO, Lakewood Ranch Business Alliance

Dedication:

This book is dedicated to Melanie Underwood, the most Valuable Leader I know.

She knows me better than I know myself.

She has cried with me in my sorrows.

She has lifted me up in prayer.

She has strengthened my faith in God.

She has believed in me when I did not believe in myself.

She is my best friend!

ACKNOWLEDGMENTS

Everyone can make a valuable impact, and there are those who go on to make an invaluable difference.

I am grateful to so many people who contributed to my debut book, *The Valuable Leader*. My book took an immense amount of work, and would not exist without the invaluable contributions of a number of incredibly thoughtful and supportive people.

First, I would like to say that everything I have, and everything I have accomplished, is because of the grace of God. Lord, you never gave up on me; you are my greatest encourager. Thank you for being my Valuable Leader!

To my mother, Margaret Sawyer: For always believing, and praying for her baby. Thank you for all the love and support you've given me. I love you, mummy!

Melanie Underwood: Melanie is not only a great friend; she's a brilliant storyteller, writer, and artist. She worked tirelessly with me, and represented and supported me at every step of the process, from conception to publication, offering insight, warnings, encouragement, and silence at all the right times. She was instrumental in getting us to a great cover, editing, and proofreading, layout, and formatting down to the final page. Thank you, Melanie; you kept me sane throughout this process, you are my #1 fan, and I could not have done this book without you!

James (Jimmy) Major: Jimmy is a gifted writer who understood everything I was trying to accomplish from day one, when he jumped in with both feet, polishing words, without losing anything important while also managing to make it more engaging. He took a leap of faith in me, and in my vision. If you are ever lucky enough to work with him, jump at the chance. Thank you, Jimmy; I am a better writer because of you!

Liz Coursen: Liz is an award-winning, 12-time author, editor, and publisher who has taken the quality of my book to a higher level through her editing, and proofreading skills. Thank you, Liz, I am so grateful you believed in my dream, and joined me on my journey to become a published author.

Betty Norlin: Betty is a published

author, educator, and writer who offered great advice, edits, and writing suggestions, all while encouraging me to write. Thank you, Betty, for not just believing in me but for knowing that I could write a book.

K. Alison Albury. Alison is a successful published author, and has witnessed my growth and transformation as a leader. It was only fitting that she be the one to pen the Foreword to my first book, *The Valuable Leader*. Thank you, Alison; I am a better person and leader because you invested time in me!

I am indebted to so many valuable leaders. To all my friends who took the time to share their stories and support for my book: Alice Sands, Barry Banther, Beatriz Barni, Beth Albury Konechne, Crystal Underwood, Debi Frock, Don Gagnon, Donna Marie Albury, Hardy Smith, Janet Avalone, Jean Claude Zidor, John Counter, John Rollins, Joseph Germain, Joy Rampello, Jesse Silva, Kathy Kasten, Kevin W. McCarthy, Lillian Knowles Cash, Melanie Underwood, Mike Harrell, Randy Keirn, Rick Kreider, Rob Smith, Roy Hindman, Stella Pinder, Steve Smith, and Yolando Torres Cox – thank you!

We are all better individuals and leaders thanks to people who have helped develop and lead us on our path. To all those who I have had the opportunity to lead, be led by, and watch as you led others from afar, thank you!

If you like this book, the credit goes to Melanie and Jimmy. Lead on!

Table of Contents

FOREWARD   1

PROLOGUE:

    The Kind of Leader Everyone Wants to Follow   3

INTRODUCTION:

    A Little Bit of Value Goes a Long Way   21

CHAPTER 1. LISTEN WELL:

    Have an Ear for the Sound of Leadership   29

CHAPTER 2. ENVISION THE FUTURE:

    Have an Eye to See the Possibilities   49

CHAPTER 3. TAKE ACTION:

    Follow Your Instincts, Go with Your Gut   65

CHAPTER 4. DEVELOP:

    Follow the Scent of Growth   87

CHAPTER 5. ENGAGE WITH OTHERS:

    Lead with a Human Touch   109

CHAPTER 6. REFLECT:

    Learn from a Taste of the Past   125

CHAPTER 7. SERVE:

    Have a Heart for Leadership, Put Others First   149

CHAPTER 8. SUMMARY:

    Now it's Your Turn, Lead On   171

ABOUT THE AUTHOR   185

NOTES   188

FOREWARD

I am so pleased to write the Foreword to this valuable book about leadership by a lady whom I have known for almost 40 years. I first met Velma Knowles in the small back office of a charitable organization in the Bahamas, when she came to apply for a job...any job. I was immediately impressed by Velma's candor, her desire to better herself, and her eagerness to learn. She was truly an "uncut diamond" who was willing to listen and learn. Those of us who worked with her marveled as Velma pursued her dreams, including a university education, entirely on her own effort. Seeing such a young person obtain her own financing, hand a straight-A report card to her sponsors every semester, and then graduate with honors, I knew Velma was going to be a true leader. Her faith and stick-to-it abilities have demonstrated that fact.

It seems so fitting that this book, *The Valuable Leader*, has been written by a leader, herself. Velma gives much insight into how each person can become a true leader and successfully interact with others who want to follow. Her personal stories and those of others are interspersed with good examples in her bullet points and chapters, all of which makes for thought-provoking reading.

Velma Knowles has always been a leader who is faith-driven and humble, despite her rise in the corporate world. *The Valuable Leader* will show these facts, and I am honored to give her accolades for such well-deserved accomplish-ments.

K. Alison Albury, Wellington, Florida
(formerly of Nassau, Bahamas)
Author, *Life on a Rock*

PROLOGUE: THE KIND OF LEADER EVERYONE WANTS TO FOLLOW

WHAT DO I KNOW ABOUT BEING A LEADER? When I began thinking of how I could share my lessons on leadership, I thought, if the truth were told, my role as a leader has taken me through a variety of twists and turns. I made so many mistakes as a leader. After all, I took a long, long time to really understand what being a leader was all about. I am thankful for the lessons from the leaders in my life. Many of these leaders provided good lessons, and others, sadly, provided poor lessons. Today I am thankful for the opportunity to share with you real-life examples of what leading looks like. These examples will demonstrate how to become a Valuable Leader: a leader who everyone wants to follow.

Friends, the real value of a leader is in the understanding of the price of leading. What is the "price" or "value" in a leader, and in leadership? Do you value your leaders, those people you report to? Do the people in your life value you as their leader? The answers to these and other questions can be found in this book, *The Valuable Leader*. Those questions cannot be answered simply because I alone have all the answers, but, rather, because this book reflects many other stories from those who also had valuable leaders in their lives.

Leading others is a priceless gift.

The Valuable Leader is about real value from real leaders told through real stories. In the pages of this book, you will learn the seven steps you can take to find greater growth, value, and influence. Let this book be your guide. The seven steps outlined here will be a source to help you answer what I believe is a question all leaders need to ask themselves. The question is this:

Am I a Valuable Leader?

Everyone is both a leader and a follower. We all have leaders in our lives. We are all leaders. But there are also those of us who do not believe that we are leaders. People generally follow two schools of thought: One side sees a leader as having an important title, position, or role; the other side believes that to be a leader you must work for a company, or own your own business. The result of this confusion is that the real meaning of a leader has been misunderstood.

This misunderstanding has come about because leaders, and leadership, have been too long associated only within the context of business.

Being a leader is more than having a title and being in business; being a leader is about living a life of value. Being a leader is about knowing your true worth. To be a leader is about making a positive difference in the lives of others. A leader values people. Period.

You are a leader. I know you are because you have decided that reading this book, *The Valuable Leader*, is important to you. Perhaps you want to find your value as a leader, confirm your value as a leader, or seek to grow from the value lived out by other leaders. Whatever your reason for reading this book, be assured you have made the right decision. You hold in your hand real value from real leaders, told through real stories.

To get the most from *The Valuable Leader*, you must stop, and consider where you are today in your growth as a leader. As a leader, think about what kind of values you live. Who do you influence because you are a leader in the lives of others?

Bottom line, friends: What kind of leader are you?

A Valuable Leader is one who lives the proven seven-step system outlined in this book. By living these seven steps, you too will become the kind of leader everyone wants to follow. Let me share a little story about how I discovered the Valuable Leader, because I want you to live your leadership from a position of value.

Once upon a time, a long time ago, I grew up in the city of Nassau on the small island of New Providence in the Bahamas. I spent my first seven years as a young adult working in Nassau before coming to the United States. I learned many lessons about leading others in those seven years, and had my first opportunity to work shoulder-to-shoulder with a Valuable Leader: Alison Albury.

Alison was a tall, slender, and strong woman, the office manager for a nonprofit conservation organization known as The Bahamas National Trust. Even though Alison did not know me well, she had a vision and believed in my potential. Alison hired me to be her office assistant. I like to say, I was the gofer. I would go for this and go for that. I was happy to do all errands for the office. I would make bank deposits (before the invention of online banking), or pick up the mail from the post office (in the islands, you go to a Post Office mailbox. Homes didn't have on-location mailboxes with on-site delivery. By the way, they still don't today.), and other similar tasks.

Alison and I worked together for three

years at the Trust, and while a person might say my position or title was of little value, I never felt that I was not valued. In fact, Alison made me feel like I was the most valued employee in the office. Not only did she invest time in my development while at the office, she also took the time to get to know me as a person outside the office. Alison knew that I was from a low-income family and did not have opportunities like her two girls, Kelly and Victoria. For me, without a high-paying job or a college education, attending certain social events in the community, like the Camperdown Stables Annual Horse Show, was just a fantasy.

One year, Alison invited me to come along with her and her family to one of the Camperdown Shows. This was my first time going to such an event, and I distinctly remember worrying about what to wear. After all, I didn't have fancy clothes, but I really wanted to go and, more than anything, I wanted to fit in. Have you ever felt like that? I didn't know anything about horses back then and, to be honest, I really didn't like horses. After all, there was the smell. But, I liked Alison. She was a woman I wanted to follow, a woman I wanted to emulate. Spending time with Alison made me feel important and, most of all, *valued.*

Well, it turns out I did attend my first horse show and many more after that. Alison never invited me out of obligation; She wanted to include me because she valued me as a person and enjoyed the time we spent together. For me, I did not go to the shows because she was my boss and I had to go. I really liked spending time with Alison and her family. A horse show also afforded me the opportunity to meet so many valuable and influential people. The experience impacted me and broadened my perspective about life and leadership. I am thankful I had a strong, influential woman like Alison early in my career, because as I look back and reflect, I have come to learn that all leaders are in the business of leading people.

One of the key values I learned from Alison was to value the people in your life.

Alison showed me that she believed that everyone has value, regardless of your social status, your title, or skill set. She was the first of many leaders in my life, and I believe she is the type of leader everyone would want to follow.

Following a successful career in the Bahamas, I traveled to the U.S. in pursuit of my education. I will uncover more revelations about my journey and development later in the book, but, needless to say, there were Valuable Leaders along the way who helped me meet my goal.

After completing my studies, and receiving my degrees in Marketing and

Management from both Webber International University and The University of Tampa, I secured positions with several organizations. Over the course of the last two decades, working in the U.S., you could say that I have seen a few leaders during my career. I have even had opportunities to step up into the role of a leader myself. With all that experience working in both the Bahamas and the U.S. for 27-plus years, I thought, "I am a leader. I know how to lead and I know what leadership is all about." My library is filled with hundreds of books about leadership, and I have read each one of them.

Looking at my 27 years' experience, you may be thinking: "Velma, you don't look a day over 30." Maybe you looked at the picture on the back cover of my book and said, "I thought she would be taller!" Well, the truth is, I am way over 30 and I can get a little bit taller when I put my heels on, but that's another story for another book.

A Valuable Leader is not defined in terms of length of years, and my leadership story is probably not much different than yours.

I remember early in my career in the U.S., when I was striving to climb the corporate ladder. My days were filled with hard work, burning the candle at both ends, and going nowhere fast! In 1993 the chance came for me to step into a leadership role. With six managers reporting to me, a large corner office with a window, a new title and a large raise, I had arrived! I was in leadership, or, so I thought.

I recall one of my first leadership moments. My team and I were in the office conference room discussing the renewal of our marketing agency contract. Joe (name changed), a marketing planner, spoke up and said he felt we would need to explore hiring another agency. The agency on record was proposing a substantial increase in fees, and Joe believed continuing with that agency would put us way over budget.

Without thinking I stood up and blurted out in a loud voice, "Joe, you are wrong! There's no need to go with another marketing agency. I will be the negotiator and get that contract renewed at last year's price or less!" I could see Joe sink down in his chair. He was embarrassed as all the other staff looked at him and then at me. My actions that day made me look like a callous person who was not a Valuable Leader. In fact I was not a leader at all, let alone one who was valuable.

The result: My team did not like me. In fact, I really did not like myself that day. My actions were not reflective of a Valuable Leader, and certainly not of a leader anyone would want to follow. If I were one of the members of my team that day, I would not have wanted to follow me either. That day, I had forgotten the lesson learned from Alison so many years before: I had forgotten that a leader is an individual who values people.

Even though I had read all those books in my library and had worked with many leaders during my international career, I still had so much more to learn about what being a leader was all about. Reading about the qualities of a leader in all those books did not mean that I had learned how to apply them. Watching all the actions of my past leaders and hearing what they had to say also did not mean I chose to practice them. We are all responsible for the choices we make in life. I was only looking at leadership from a business perspective. I missed out on the fact that leadership is everywhere. Being a leader is about being a person who values people!

I was a leader in the eyes of the executives I worked for, in the positions held, and in the responsibilities that I had, but not in eyes of the people who reported to me. Not in the eyes of the team I was supposed to be leading. After all, being a leader means people follow you, right? But do they follow you because they *have* to, or because they *want* to?

Jim Rohn, an American entrepreneur, author, motivational speaker, and philosopher who left an indelible legacy of time-proven principles once said:

"The challenge of leadership is to be strong, but not rude; be kind, but not weak; be bold, but not a bully; be thoughtful, but not lazy; be humble, but not timid; be proud, but not arrogant; show humor, not folly."

People often say that experience is the best teacher, but if we experience life and never learn from our experiences, we are none the better for having lived that life. When we examine our life experiences, then we are able to learn, and become a better person, live a better life, and be a better leader.

Being a leader is not only relevant in business but also in life. Leadership is not only about the position; leadership is about the value a leader brings to the position. A leader is not defined by a title but is defined by the way he or she lives life. Valuing others and knowing your own value is a way of life for the Valuable Leader.

Leaders are people who live the values that make their presence invaluable. They are so valuable to their organization, to their family, to their community, that everyone wants to follow them.

I learned the hard way that having the title of leader does not mean you know anything about leadership.

Being a leader has everything to do with being valuable. That's exactly why I created this book, *The Valuable Leader: A seven-step guide to greater growth, value, and influence.* I want to share the values I have learned with other leaders like you. I believe this book will carve out a path to help you lead yourself and your teams. Whether you are a seasoned leader or an emerging leader who has just begun your journey, you have value. *The Valuable Leader* is packed with real stories about real leaders who lead others with real value.

How are you writing your story? Are you a Valuable Leader?

Your leadership journey is yours, and, with these seven steps, you can begin your own path towards finding value. If you have been leading for years, you can rediscover the value in leading others. As an emerging leader, you can learn and apply leadership lessons from examples of how others have led. *The Valuable Leader* is for everyone who truly wants to lead with value because being a leader of value is the highest level of leadership.

I have come to believe that the hardest person you will ever lead in your life and in your business is yourself. Friends, to lead others, you must first learn to lead yourself. As a Valuable Leader you must value *you*. You must know your real worth. Throughout the remaining pages of this book we will begin walking the path together. This path will take us on an in-depth look at each of the seven steps to becoming a Valuable Leader.

I know, for me, if I could blame the person responsible for the majority of my leadership problems, the guilt would be too heavy for me to carry, because I would have to blame myself. "Being a great leader comes after you have learned to be a great follower," was a lesson that took me a long time to learn. Learning to lead yourself means that you have learned to be a great follower. Only a leader who has followed well knows how to lead others well!

Thomas J. Watson, who served as the chairman and CEO of International Business Machines (IBM) and shepherded the company's growth into an international force from 1914 to 1956 said,

"Nothing so conclusively proves a man's ability to lead others as what he does from day to day to lead himself."

How true.

You are the most important person that you will ever lead. When you can lead yourself well, you earn the right to lead a large number of people.

To become the kind of leader everybody wants to follow, you must first start with you, and begin by learning to value yourself. When you learn to value yourself you understand that your life is a priceless, and valued, gift.

People often loosely use the word "leadership" in business and life. Parents are thought to lead their children. Executives are thought to lead their businesses. In fact, anyone who holds a distinguished title or position is thought to be a leader. But what does leadership really look like? What are the qualities that make up a real leader?

Allow me to illustrate the concept by sharing a story of an individual who was a great example of a Valuable Leader in my life.

In July of 2013 I witnessed real leadership qualities when I traveled home to Nassau. I went home to spend a few months with my Aunt Winifred, or "Aunt Winnie" as she was affectionately known. During those months in the summer of 2013, I learned what leadership really looks like, and what real qualities one must live out daily to be a true Valuable Leader.

John Maxwell, my mentor and an American author, speaker, and pastor, has written many books on leadership. John, who has been voted to be the number one leadership and management guru by *Inc.*

magazine, says this about leadership:

"Leadership is influence, nothing more, nothing less."

John's statement might sound too simple to be true, but he is right. You see, no one influenced me more in leadership than my Aunt Winnie.

You might ask, why? Well, Aunt Winnie had a really simple approach to living, an approach that demonstrated the true qualities of leadership, an approach that showed me the true value of a leader.

First, let me tell you a little about my Aunt Winnie. She grew up on a small island, seven miles wide and 21 miles long. Aunt Winnie never married, never had children of her own, and never held a leadership position, or owned a large company. In fact, she worked hard as a sales clerk for over 50 years.

Aunt Winnie never earned any college degrees. Her education stopped in the sixth grade when she began working to help her mother pay the family bills. She never knew the feeling of owning a home or having people working for her. How could Aunt Winnie be a leader? She was a leader because she influenced me tremendously, and "leadership is influence, nothing more, nothing less."

You are probably asking how did she

lead? I am glad you asked. Leadership was consistently evident in Aunt Winnie's life. She demonstrated four key leadership traits, living each of them out day-to-day.

Be a *listener* – You could tell Aunt Winnie anything and know that she was listening to you. She had a welcoming smile that said, in a silent voice, "Tell me what's on your mind." She was always interested in what you had to say. Anyone who spoke with her always enjoyed his or her conversation. Aunt Winnie taught me that a strong quality of leadership is listening to others with an understanding ear. You always had 100 percent of her attention.

Be an *encourager* – Aunt Winnie was the consummate cheerleader. She was a tremendous encourager, constantly telling me how proud she was of me. Her quality of encouraging others was even more on display in the three months I spent with her when, at age 69, she was diagnosed with cancer. Even as I watched her fight for her life, she encouraged me to live each day to the fullest.

Be *authentic* – Sometimes, when we are in leadership roles, we think we must act a certain way. Aunt Winnie showed me that a true quality of leadership is when you are your authentic self. I think I loved her authenticity the most: she was real. Aunt Winnie never judged; instead, she accepted you just the way you were. She was consistently consistent, authentically authentic.

Be *dedicated* – Leadership has been around for centuries, and we all have different thoughts that come to mind when we hear the word. But Aunt Winnie knew that leadership was about dedication. She was totally dedicated to her family, her friends, and her job. Aunt Winnie's dedication wasn't a secret. Everyone who knew her knew the truth: she was dedicated.

There are many qualities that could best describe leadership. Take a moment, and go online and ask the search engine Google to look up Warren Bennis. A scholar, advisor to American presidents, and an author, regarded as a pioneer in the contemporary field of leadership studies, Bennis said:

"Becoming a leader is synonymous with becoming yourself. It is precisely that simple and also that difficult."

Real qualities of leadership are the ones lived out day after day, by ordinary people like you. Like Aunt Winnie. Perhaps you have an Aunt Winnie in your life, or maybe you are that person to someone. Either way, I challenge you today to develop leadership as a way of life by practicing these four traits:

Be a Listener to understand

Be an Encourager to lift up others

Be Authentic to be who you are

Be Dedicated to serve others

The keywords learned from Aunt Winnie form the acronym LEAD. Aunt Winnie demonstrated these LEAD qualities, and, because her example taught me so well, I have built many strong and lasting relationships. She helped me see the value in my ability to lead, and to see the value in me.

Who are the Valuable Leaders in your life? How about yourself? Are you a Valuable Leader to others? When was the last time you looked in a mirror and asked yourself this question: Would I work for me? Am I the kind of leader who I would want to work with?

Begin your review.

You have read Chapter 1; let's take a moment to apply what you have learned. Take a few minutes to evaluate how you commonly present yourself as a leader. Take out a piece of paper, or use the Notes page at the back of this book and write out your answers to the following questions:

1.   What are your leadership traits?

2.   Who are the people in your life who *want* to follow you, not *have* to? List at least

three people.

3. Based on your performance today, would you consider yourself a Valuable Leader? If yes, why? If no, why not?

Unleash Your Value!

The process of actually increasing your value as a leader can be daunting, and a lot of leaders give up before reaching their full potential.

Are you ready to become a more Valuable Leader?

View my exclusive video series and learn more about how you can increase your value as a leader with my proven seven-step process.

Get started at **TheValuableLeader.com**.

INTRODUCTION: A LITTLE BIT OF VALUE GOES A LONG WAY

Are you a Valuable Leader? Do you know what you need to lead in today's dynamic environment? As a leader you have a dual role: you must lead yourself and lead your teams. There are seven steps that will help you improve your leadership – in your business, and in your everyday life.

Today's leaders are on a journey to discover or refresh their understanding of the tools they need to lead. Whether you are a seasoned leader or an emerging one, building the foundation for you to lead tomorrow must start today.

In this book you will focus on the following key takeaways:

Your growth – identify the seven qualities to becoming the Valuable Leader.

Your value – uncover leadership traits needed to lead others through value.

Your influence – recognize the foundation for successful leaders.

There is an old saying: "You can't export products you don't produce." In other words, you can't give what you don't have.

That's why I wrote this book. I could not have done something like this before, and at this moment even as I write, I know that completing a book takes a village. I am not writing *The Valuable Leader* because I know everything about being a leader. I am writing the book because I know so many people have Valuable Leaders in their lives and that this book gives us all a vehicle to share our stories. I want to give you a word of advice that I wish I'd had a long time ago: It's never too late to rediscover the value you have in life and in business. You are a Valuable Leader; you may only need a little reminder and reinforcement to dust off those qualities you know you have inside. Maybe all you need is to sharpen those skills once again so that you can move forward on your path to becoming priceless.

Are you ready to dig deep into your own life, into your own DNA? Being a Valuable Leader must become your way of life. A Valuable Leader is not something you do; a Valuable Leader is someone you become. When you lead by valuing others, you have become the best leader you can be.

Maybe you have thought, "I am the best leader I have ever been. I am leading large multi-billion dollar corporations, and hundreds, even thousands, of people report to me. If this is not leadership, then what is?"

This is exactly what a lot of "leaders" think. I know, because while I did not lead multi-billion-dollar corporations and manage thousands, or even hundreds of people in my little corner of corporate America and the years working in the Bahamas, I thought I knew how to lead. *Wrong.* Through years of self-discovery and real-life learning I have learned the difference between a status quo leader of a large corporation or large groups of people, and a true Valuable Leader. *The Valuable Leader* will help you to discover, or rediscover, and learn to apply the seven steps to greater growth, value, and influence.

Every day, I work to be a better leader, because I know the kind of leader I used to be. Today, my leadership journey has come a long way, and, guess what, my quest continues. After all, leadership is a process: you never "arrive." Being a leader is like what John Wooden, head coach at Indiana State and UCLA and the most successful coach in the history of college basketball, once said:

"It's what you know *after* you know it all

that truly counts."

Leaders are learners and life is about learning from lessons, so we don't have to continue to retake the test.

Stop and think for a moment. In today's world, we don't always pause, take a step back, and take time to think. Let's pause here and take a moment; please play along with me. What's the most valuable possession you have? Maybe you are thinking, "My most valuable possession is my car; after all, I drive a fancy one." Or maybe you are thinking, "No, my home is the most valuable; after all, it cost hundreds of thousands of dollars." There are so many things you could think of and hopefully you are thinking, because, well, thinking appears to be a lost art these days. Take another moment and think a little more and complete this sentence: "The most valuable possession I have is _____" (you fill in the blank).

Wow! That was not an easy exercise, right? There are other questions like this that we all need to stop and think about. When we pause, ponder, and think, we find real value in our life and in our leadership. I could go on and on, but your time is too valuable, so let me get to the point.

Let me suggest to you that the most valuable possession you have is your life. In short, your most valuable possession is *you!*

I took a long time to realize that the most valuable possession in my own life was just that – my life. Maybe you are like me, or you are smarter than me and have already discovered your most valuable possession. Either way, stopping and thinking is a good exercise because knowing something does not mean much if you and I don't do something to apply that knowledge.

As I think back on my time growing up in Nassau, I don't really recall thinking I was valuable. Please don't misunderstand me. I *was* loved.

My mom was a loving, hardworking, and humble woman, and she took really good care of my siblings and me. You could say she gave all she had for her children.

My father was a fun, outgoing guy who had a captivating smile. He could get along with anyone, and he did to his own detriment. He died at the age of 36, when I was eight years old. Losing my dad seems like only yesterday.

The absence of my dad created a void in me. Today I realize that I missed out on something valuable. That something was having a loving father in my life.

Feeling that I lacked value was not

because of something my family did or did not do. The feelings were mine, not theirs. These feelings were something I needed to deal with and yet, I never knew how to deal with them. Looking back, I don't think I was ever aware of feeling I lacked value until much later in life. I did not place value on people, as I should have. In my mind a leader's value could only be found by holding a large title, or an important position with a large company. You may recall from the previous chapter, when I began my career working for Alison, I did not hold what I thought was an important position or work for a large company. While my job at The Bahamas National Trust did afford me a large office and important title, the experience taught me that people, not titles, are the real value in life and business.

My experience seeded a need in me and put me on a mission to find value, in both life and in business. My quest was to become a Valuable Leader, a person who others would want to follow.

Time has taught me that you can't give away what you don't have. I could not give value in my business life, to my team members or to myself, because I did not feel like I had value in my personal life. It took me a long time before I discovered I had a blind spot in my life, and even a much longer time for me to bridge that gap. The people I worked with over the years each taught me values that impacted my personal life. Today, I am excited to say that I am on that path and I have found the value inside myself. I am valuable, both in life and in business. Today, I want the same for you. You have before you an opportunity that will reconfirm, rediscover, or rebirth your value. You are on the pathway to becoming the Valuable Leader you were born to be.

Join me over the next few pages as we uncover real value. I will take you through each step and you will see how real people showed real value through real stories. You will unwrap your value from a personal perspective, from a business standpoint, and from a leader's outlook. Let's lead on!

Uncover Your Blind Spots.

Finding your blind spots doesn't have to be a difficult process, as long as you are armed with a proven system to detect them. My coaching sessions will help you see what you're missing, and grow as a Valuable Leader.

Find out how coaching can help you in my exclusive video series. Go to **TheValuableLeader.com**.

CHAPTER 1. LISTEN WELL: HAVE AN EAR FOR THE SOUND OF LEADERSHIP

"The ear of the leader must ring with the voices of the people."

— Woodrow Wilson

HOW MANY TIMES HAVE YOU FELT THAT YOUR LEADER WAS NOT LISTENING TO YOU? Better yet, how many times have you been so busy that you did not listen to someone who needed your attention? If you are like me, you would agree, we are guilty! To listen is defined as "To hear something with thoughtful attention: to give consideration."

The first step on your path to becoming a Valuable Leader is to LISTEN. Valuable leaders *listen.*

I wish that we could all say we listen and, for that matter, listen well. We were given two ears and one mouth for a reason. Perhaps you will agree, you spend more of your time thinking of what you will say when the other person stops talking, than listening to what that person is actually saying. We are all guilty of this, but the question is, will you admit your guilt? This was something I needed to learn to do. I needed to admit that I was guilty of not listening. I was guilty of not hearing others with thoughtful attention.

In real life, we think that we know what's being said, but we don't stop to clarify the conversation before jumping to unhelpful conclusions.

When we learn the art of listening, of putting others before ourselves, of giving thoughtful consideration to what others are saying, we become a Valuable Leader. We take a step on our path forward because we have learned to appreciate others. By taking the time to listen we improve our relationships, have a better understanding of each other, and reduce confusion.

To become a Valuable Leader, you must first learn to listen and, more than that, to listen well.

To learn to listen well means that you actually stop and listen to others, not solely hearing what they say. You learn to value what they say, why they are saying it, and what it truly means. Words can say one thing, but mean something else. Non-verbal clues can override a person's verbal communication. We have all read the research, which, indicates that we get most of our clues of the intent behind a person's words from non-verbal sources. If there appears to be a conflict between the two then, we believe the non-verbal every time. This may sound like a cliché, but "it's not *what* you say but *how* you say it." When we as leaders don't take the time to actually listen, we can make an array of major mistakes!

I come from the association world. I have spent over two decades working inside organizations that have members. We existed for the members, so I learned quickly that a key element of our success in membership growth, retention, and experience was to listen to our members.

The same is true for any organization. As leaders, you need to listen to your customers. And as a woman who considers herself a lifelong student, I have come to value the role an employee plays in serving an organization. Listening to your employees helps you build a culture that serves your customers and members well. For our members, and our teams, we must think about what they are saying. We must be sure we listen and take action from their feedback. This is a lesson I learned early in my career when I went to work for an organization with over four million members.

I remember our association membership was down. The deficit was about 90,000 members. The Chief Operating Officer (COO), John, tagged me to chair the membership retention taskforce. Our purpose was to find a way to recover the membership deficiency so we could meet our growth goals. I thought to myself, "This is either a great steppingstone towards my career growth or, if I fail, this could be a career-limiting move."

Thankfully, the answer was the former, not the latter. John knew that to find the answers needed to solve this member deficit problem, a team effort was required. He would have to listen to the recommendations from those who were not in so-called leadership positions. John would have to take a risk and listen to what his employees thought were the best next steps.

John asked me to lead the team, something I had never done before. I immediately began reaching out to the people I believed could help with this challenge. The situation required a team that listened to the issues and to each other. This was my opportunity to lead. I knew that great leaders pull together the collective wisdom of others and work together. Listening to each other and collaborating ensured that everyone felt valued and all ideas were heard. When each member on a team feels valued, the performance of the team is elevated and the challenges facing the team are overcome.

In any association, when the leaders envision the success of their organization, they know that membership is not a department. Membership is everyone's job. Our cross-functional team came together, reaching into many departments, and listening to their ideas. The team dug deep through various mounds of data and asked the questions "why" or "why not." The team saw obstacles as opportunities and, in the end, created a successful member retention plan.

To put the plan into action, buy-in was needed from every member of the team. Endorsement by consensus is a critical part of any successful plan. Endorsement by consensus ensures people on the team are included and feel understood, considered, and respected. An atmosphere of camaraderie and a culture of cooperation are created. The team listened to each individual contribution and created the plan for moving forward.

The result: Not only did the association make up the 90,000-member deficit, we also gained an additional 10,000 members. The turn-around added a total of 100,000 members! This result was a combination of many people learning to listen to each other. Regardless of where we were in the organization, everyone respected each other enough to listen to what each of us had to say.

Not all teams listen well enough to reap results like the team in my story. However, results can be achieved when the leaders in the organization value the individuals enough to listen to them. I remember the team members having open minds and listening to the ideas of their fellow associates. When we presented our recommendations, the executive leadership group was open and listened to the team's recommendations, knowing that a handful of those ideas were untested. The association's COO had the vision to believe in his team enough to listen to solutions that the team felt would make the difference.

Sometimes, organizations expect leaders to be the ones with the answers. However, great leaders know that they don't have all the answers. Great leaders are aware and see that everyone has value, and that learning to listen to your team will make you a better leader. Listening takes time, especially when team members can be located across the company, across departments, and across geographical locations. Investing the time to listen is worth every minute because everyone has value and there is value in learning to listen well.

How well do you listen?

We live in a world where there are many

devices available to help us connect. We have portable computers, iPads and tablets, smart phones and so much more, much to the credit of Steve Jobs, co-founder of Apple Inc., and Bill Gates, principal founder of Microsoft Corporation. Even with all this technology, leaders seem to struggle to really connect with their teams, family, or community.

Technology is here! We are connected instantaneously and physical boundaries are eliminated. The rise of the global workforce opens the doors for businesses and challenges for leaders. To remain competitive, leaders must find ways to network with others. The leader's teams, business partners, other leaders, and customers/members all provide a competitive force that leaders can leverage to win. However, relationships are more about interacting with others, which is best done when leaders listen.

Our high-tech world has brought many benefits, like immediate access, instant knowledge (ask Google) worldwide travel, and so on. But because we live in an instantaneous world, we have become impatient. This impatience has transferred over to our relationships, and we appear to have a shorter attention span. We don't wait for a person to speak – we finish his or her sentences. Our focus has become blurred with less effort spent to truly connect and attentively listen.

I, like you, have heard this statement before, "You are just not listening to me." We feel ignored when our leaders (or anybody, for that matter) don't listen to us. Leaders who take the time to listen understand the importance of being valued.

Poor listening leads to breakdowns in communication, breakups in relationships, and overall conflict in the workplace or home. The cost of not listening runs into billions of dollars for companies and destroys many families and relationships. Look at the level of conflict in your workplace or in your life. I know personally the results of poor listening skills. But I know too that you can get better. I am in no way where I need to be, but I am far better than I used to be. Here are a few tips on how to listen well that I have learned from other leaders who have added value to my life:

Be expressive when you listen.

Look into the eyes of the person when you are listening.

Ask questions to gain greater under-standing.

Have you heard the phrase "The world does not revolve around you"? This was an in-your-face message that one of my managers once said to me. His message hurt me and for sure was not the best example of how to speak to your employee, but, after much reflection, I realized that my manager was trying to help me. Eventually I learned that what he was really saying to me was "get outside of yourself and focus on others first." After all, not everything was all about me. A Valuable Leader generally earns his or her value in the same way one earns respect. Notice I said, "earns." Only when your focus shifts from self to others will you begin to truly listen and to really value.

What does this mean for leaders? Have you ever been at your desk or walking down the hall at the office and your leader walked right by you and did not even speak a word to you? To be a leader who listens, we must be willing to speak up and connect with others. We must seek them out and engage them to get them to share. We learn as leaders when we listen to others, when we value them so much that we use our ability to listen with an understanding ear, and we should never miss an opportunity to do so, even if we are merely walking down the hall or through the office.

I ask you: Is leadership showing up in your life? Do you value what others think or what they say enough to reach out and connect with them? Effective leaders are the ones who value the act of listening. There has been so much written about the role of communication, the need for communication, and how to improve team performance through better communication skills. I agree with this focus and perhaps you do too. You could even make the argument that communication is the most important tool that a leader must have. Yet, too often communication is viewed as the art of speaking. Listening is the real value that communication brings.

Leaders should practice active listening as "a strength" to connect more with others. People want to be heard. People feel valued when they know that their leaders are interested enough in them to listen to what they have to say.

Dr. Stephen Covey, an educator, keynote speaker, and an author well known for his book *The Seven Habits of Highly Effective People,* gives us the great reminder to:

"Seek first to understand, then to be understood."

The leader who values listening is one who makes mental notes or jots down key phrases on a piece of paper about what the other person is saying.

I value listening as a key tool in leadership so much that I try very hard to practice to listen first and then think of how I can best respond. Do I listen well all the time? Sadly, the answer is no. But, a leader who listens is one who is constantly focused on learning to listen. When a person is speaking, leaders must set the example to listen to what that person is saying. The power of focus will give value to a leader when he or she listens. We must all keep in mind that listening skills, like leadership skills, can be learned and improved over time. Over time, you will sharpen your ears to listen to what others are saying versus merely hearing what they said.

The value of listening to others is something I have experienced first-hand from my friend Jean Claude. I met Jean Claude while attending a local church in Tampa. He was always smiling and wanting to know how things were going with my family in the Bahamas and with me. Jean Claude always made me feel so valued and I often wondered why he always took the time to stop and listen to me. So, when the time came for me to think of a way I could share the power of listening with you, I thought I would ask my friend Jean Claude. He related a very powerful story of a leader who embodied the value of listening.

In the mid '90s, Jean Claude was in his senior year at Lycée Pinchinat de Jacmel in Haiti. The authorities from the department of education wanted to implement changes in the leadership of the school. To that end they brought in a new principal who was a teacher from a well-regarded learning institution in the city. There was a drastic transformation in students' behaviors as a result of the simple but so powerful interventions and changes. Jean Claude tells how this complete transformation came to be.

Often Haitian parents took the wrong way with the right intentions in the discipline of their children. The school system also did things the wrong way but with good intentions. Teachers at that time were a direct reflection of Haitian societal beliefs. The thought was that with "baton whipping," a child's negative behavior would be corrected. Thus, Mr. L., a man in his thirties, 260 pounds, six foot two, five-day-a-week body builder-type, was brought in. Mr. L.'s personality was strong and he was charged with discipline for the entire school.

Each day, Mr. L. would patrol all four corners of the school with his whip "rigwaz" to keep everything in so-called order. Did anyone really respect or fear him? Perhaps the fear was nothing but that of receiving one of his abusive whippings. The reality was that, because of his "whippings," hundreds of students dropped out or were kicked out of the school every year. Why? I would suggest because the students were in direct opposition to the school's archaic and abusive rules. Most of them, after dropping out, abandoned school and therefore augmented the already high number of delinquent adolescents on the streets. The lack of leadership had failed the students.

One early fall day a new leader entered the picture, Mr. D. He was not afraid of taking action that was contrary to the prevailing Haitian beliefs. Mr. D. took the stance that there would be no more whippings. He believed that the power of listening and constant dialogue would make a positive impact in the hearts and minds of the young students. Hence, every day, before raising the flag, he religiously listened and spoke with the rising sea of students, all dressed in khaki pants and white shirts.

His first speech reminded students that this school was his alma mater and that he considered himself a successful individual giving back to his community. He had even taken a pay cut to devote his time and energy to this worthy, educational, and life-changing cause. His voice spoke of a future where the school's next generation depended on open dialogues and choices they made today. For the first time, the students felt that their voices would be heard; someone was listening and cared about them and their education. Gone was the feeling of simply going to school to go to school. Instead, the students felt that they were going to school to become better prepared, well-educated, and useful citizens.

Mr. D. used examples from the glorious passages of Haiti's history to instill a sense of patriotism, and each powerful and inspirational morning dialogue awakened the students. His listening skills had gained him the support of the student body and put the authoritarian principal out of a job.

The art of listening and having a dialogue using words accomplished so easily that which the whip could not. The change was very evident under the new leadership: students' grades and passing percentage rate surged during class and on official tests. The school regained the confidence of the community, and the number of students attending the school doubled in a couple of years. The student body became united while developing a spirit of belonging. This unity continues today among the students scattered all over the world serving communities in a variety of fields.

This powerful lesson early in Jean Claude's life made a valuable impression. He listened and learned from that experience. Today, each year, he gives to that same community just as his principal, Mr. D., did. Each year, Jean Claude leads a volunteer team to Jacmel, for a two-week youth summer camp. The camp also includes a four-day mobile clinic, which travels into remote areas of the country, where an average of 1,200 patients receive care and medications.

Using the art of listening and dialogue with proven leadership skills, Jean Claude continues to do what the whip could not. He positively impacts others' lives to make the world a better place to live together in dignity.

After listening to Jean Claude's story, I have a better understanding of why he cared enough about me to listen to me. His value of listening to others is a direct result of the value that he received back in his school days, back when a new leader came to his school and came with an ear to listen. This is where Jean Claude learned the power of listening, and today he continues to go back to where his learning all began. He goes back to Haiti to listen to the needs of others, because that's where someone first listened to him.

The second story is from a newfound friend, Rick Kreider. I met Rick at a local Toastmasters club meeting. Within seconds of meeting Rick, he and I became friends. Maybe we became friends because we both spent many years in corporate America, or maybe because we both share a strong faith in our Creator. Either way, I knew that there was something about Rick that I admired. I couldn't quite put my finger on what I admired, but I respected him so much in such a short period of time that I invited him to share a story about a leader in his life. Rick immediately thought of his father.

Rick's father was his mentor. His father was a very hard-working man who would put in long hours at the Philadelphia Naval Shipyard overseeing government projects. The projects required him to be involved both mentally and physically. Those projects meant making sure his team got every task completed within the required time constraints.

Rick recalls how impressed he was to witness first-hand the respect his father and his team had for one another as they worked in unison, helping one another to achieve their goals. During this time, his father always found the time to teach the team responsibilities and was always open to listen and receive any feedback. He listened no matter the source, whether from his team members and stakeholders or even outsiders. He had a listening ear and sought out feedback that would help ease the load and speed up the task at hand.

Rick also worked at the Naval Yard, but he was in a different division than his father. His father worked in the radar sector, and Rick worked in the weapons division. Shortly after he started, Rick was asked to oversee the apprentices within his division and to help mentor them into technicians. At the age of 23 he found this flattering but also surprising, since he had no formal education in leading! He never went to college nor had he taken any formal training courses in that area. But Rick said, "What the heck, let's give it a try"; besides, he always had his father nearby to bounce things off of.

After getting a few pointers from his father and viewing a few online leadership seminars, Rick thought, "I am ready to take on this leadership role – full steam ahead!" Not long after making that statement, Rick was derailed and started to doubt his ability to become a leader. Rick decided to hit the pause button and start back at the beginning. He spoke with his father again and took several formal online courses. From his training, Rick discovered he wasn't being a listener. He was not listening to the people he was being asked to lead. He realized that he had to take time and get to know his team.

Rick recalls, "What I had witnessed in my father's team years before was over 25 years worth of camaraderie that had been built up though listening and interacting." Rick was only in his first month. With his new approach in mind, Rick set out to take the time to meet with each team member. To listen and find out what all his team members strengths and weakness really were. What likes and dislikes did they have, and where did they envision themselves in a couple of years?

Having spent time listening, Rick felt he had a better understanding on how to move forward. He had a better understanding of how to pair up teams and who would better work together in the team. His listening gained him an understanding of which employees he could count on to take the lead and complete their task, and those who might need a little nudge to get things done.

Rick's lesson proved invaluable. He learned that for a leader to be effective he or she must always take the time to listen and understand his team. He needed to learn that leaders must empower teams and let the members make decisions. He learned that everyone had ideas and what people wanted most was to contribute their ideas to the success of the task at hand. By doing things like this, taking time to listen and learn, Rick had a team that was working in unison. Rick had a team that was respectful of each other, a team modeling the same camaraderie he had witnessed before, the same level of interaction and teamwork he admired in the past from watching his father's team.

I am not surprised that Rick's father was such a Valuable Leader, one who would listen to others and build strong camaraderie. I'm also not surprised to learn that Rick today carries on those same qualities of listening and learning to value others.

So I ask you the same question that I have asked myself about listening: "How can I continue to put the art of listening into practice on a daily basis? How can I improve my listening skills?" Samples of the techniques I have learned to use on my path are outlined below:

1. Ask questions, and then listen to the

answer with an understanding ear.

2.   Get comfortable with silence. Listening is the key to understanding.

3.   Give feedback and be sincere and kind when doing so. Listening shows how much you value the other person.

On to step 2!

Listening Beats Hearing.

There is a huge difference between hearing and listening. Are you ready to take the next step on your path to becoming a better listener?

My video series will introduce you to a process that works for developing your listening skills. Get started. Watch now, and learn more about workshops I conduct that will help you listen and communicate to connect.

Watch my video series at
TheValuableLeader.com.

CHAPTER 2. ENVISION THE FUTURE: HAVE AN EYE TO SEE THE POSSIBILITIES

"Some men see things as they are and ask why. Others dream things that never were and ask why not."

— George Bernard Shaw

DO YOU SEE YOUR GLASS AS HALF FULL OR HALF EMPTY? Leaders look to the future with an eye for the possibilities. A Valuable Leader has vision, and he or she imagines what could be. Leaders see tomorrow today. To envision something is defined as "to think of something that you believe might exist or happen in the future: to picture something in your mind."

The second step on your path to

becoming a Valuable Leader is to ENVISION the future. Valuable leaders have *vision!*

When it comes to having vision, I believe that we have lost the art of strategic planning – going from plans to action, casting a vision of what must be done to move us from merely setting goals to actually achieving them; from resource allocation to resource empowerment.

To envision means that as leaders we see the possibilities.

Are you a leader of the future? This was a question I asked myself on my path to becoming a Valuable Leader. After years of doing leadership all wrong, deep down inside I felt a burning desire to make change; I needed to do leadership right. To be the leader I knew I could be. To turn my head, adjust my sightlines and look forward to the future, as opposed to backward to the past. Yes, we do learn from our past, what we did right or wrong, but perhaps at this specific stage on my journey I knew that I needed to see the future: the future leader that I could be.

Perhaps you are there today, in that same place I was. Maybe you have been a leader for a long time. As a seasoned businessperson, you have "arrived," as we say. Or maybe you are the emerging leader, starting your leadership journey. Either way, there is value that comes from envisioning the future. Vision is about seeing what could be and believing in the reality of that vision happening. I believe that your vision should be to become a leader who values the future – the what could be – the leader who envisions the potential and looks forward to moving people, companies, and families from where they are to where they want and need to go.

Future leaders cannot predict the future, but they know that there is value in the collective thinking of others: they know that data can tell you stories to help you see the possibilities. And yes, they also know that they can make the world a better place. The future does not have to be like the past or the present. This statement helps to illustrate the power of vision. A wise sage once said: "Without vision, people perish." Perish the thought that we would ever believe that we are so nearsighted that we cannot envision a better tomorrow. People – customers, family, and employees – want to follow leaders who have vision. Leaders who envision and see possibilities, even when faced with obstacles. Leaders who seek solutions and don't dwell on problems.

We all remember Henry Ford, the American business magnate and founder of the Ford Motor Company. Mr. Ford would say something like this: "You can have any color Model T you want, as long as it is black." I love this reference because one could have labeled Mr. Ford a leader without vision. After all, could he not see that his customers would want other colors, like blue or red cars or whatever their favorite color was? Yet, I would argue that he did envision the future possibilities. At the time, he was focused on more than only the Model T's color; he was focused on a much larger vision. Mr. Ford was envisioning the world with an automobile for every family: a world where the car was a mode of transportation affordable to all. Most people did not see Mr. Ford's vision for the future. They saw the Ford automobile simply as a new invention only available to the rich and famous. The rest of the world, through the eyes of Mr. Ford's skeptics, only envisioned the then-current world. We have come a long way from the Model T only available in black, all because one man was a leader who valued the quality of envisioning the future.

Your ability to envision the possibilities is a compass that can help you to see others as they were made to be. People want leaders who have a better future in mind, who believe that all things are possible.

You can take the second step as the Valuable Leader. You can start right this moment. Take time to imagine. See in your mind what you want. Focus and bring clarity to that vision. Only when you can clearly see your vision do you know what could be. Share your vision with others, and, through the power of connection, you can work to achieve a future full of new opportunities. Believe in yourself and others will believe in you.

As you get to know me you will see that we are more alike than different. We both want to be better leaders, we both want to learn and grow, and we are both searching for a better life for ourselves and those we love. One of the things that might make us a little different is that I am a birder. That's what the majority of the world would call a "bird watcher." I know what you are thinking: "Velma, what do birds have to do with being a Valuable Leader?" We will dig deeper into how birding became a part of my life in another chapter; for this moment, let's focus on the value of envisioning the future.

Every year I always plan for a few birding adventures, trips where I get to forge new paths in search of my feathered friends. While there is a lot of research involved in my trips, a task I do not particularly enjoy, one of the things I do enjoy is dreaming about the trip. I take my mind and imagine what my trip will be like when I am there. How many new bird species will I see to add to my life list? What new adventures will I experience? What new people, even potential life-long friends, will I meet while I am out birding? When I envision my birding trip, I use the dream to bring the future into focus. Maybe for you, your dream was about when you would have your first child, or got your first job, your first promotion, or whatever bold idea you were having with all the expectations that dreaming brings. A leader who envisions the future also dreams, and leads with the expectation of great adventures, tremendous achievements.

Your capacity to imagine and share your future opportunities with others is a value that followers treasure. People want adventure. There are people who want more risk and danger, while others want more certainty and assurance of success. Regardless, the truth of the matter is that leaders want followers. To be a leader that others want to follow, not solely one that they have to follow, you must be a leader who knows the value of vision. You must be a leader that others value.

The activity of being a forward-looking leader is a vital distinction between those who lead and those who don't. When we take time to dream, to envision what is possible, we can be the catalyst that gives others a better future too.

When I think of a person who was a leader with vision, a man who had a clear vision of the future, a better future, I remember the father of my very dear friend, Melanie Underwood. Melanie's father, Wayde Underwood, was a leader who imagined the possibilities; he was a leader who sought to succeed against unimaginable odds. As a leader he envisioned his two daughters' potential for a better future. Wayde was exactly the visionary leader that his youngest daughter needed.

Melanie's "daddy," as she affectionately called him, was an insurance salesman who drove the breezy streets of Nassau, going door-to-door to see his clients. Back then, premiums were primarily paid in cash, so Wayde would have to drive to the customer's home and collect payments. Wayde was a dedicated father to his two young daughters – one eight, the other four. Melanie shares: "My daddy was determined to do everything he could to provide for us, we were his 'two favorite girls'." Wayde had so many dreams for his girls, but the future did not look so bright for his youngest daughter because she was born with cerebral palsy. As Melanie recalls, "The doctors held little hope that my sister would have anything resembling a normal life; in fact, they had initially declared my sister would be 'a vegetable,' not be able to move on her own."

Still, Wayde was determined to give his little girl the normal life the doctors could not promise. Every non-working moment, he would work tirelessly to teach her exercises to strengthen her weak muscles. Even at four years old, his daughter still lacked the muscle strength to walk. Melanie's daddy's dream, his vision of the future, was simply to see his precious daughter walk. Unfortunately, the small government-run physical therapy program alone was not working.

Her dad imagined a solution to better help his daughter. He strung up two ropes from each side of the living room. His daughter could use them to hold on to as she tried to pull herself upright and walk. He would stand beside her in case she stumbled, and the ropes would allow her to hold on and remain stabilized. She would pull herself along and take one step at a time with her dad's help.

Day after day he worked with her, determined that she would one day be able to walk on her own. There were people who said to him, "You are being too hard on her; she's too sick to do this." But he was determined. All he wanted was for her to be able walk on her own.

Each day her strength grew, step by step, inch by inch. Then a life-changing day happened: Wayde's little girl finally let go and took those first independent steps all on her own! She was walking, as tears of joy welled up in her daddy's eyes. He picked up

Melanie's sister, looked into her blue eyes, and gave her a big bear hug. "You did it! You did it! I *knew* you could do it. Daddy is so proud of you!"

Because of a father's faith, spirit of determination, and constant encouragement, his daughter was able to walk. He never gave up; he pressed on and followed his vision, his dream. Today his daughter is 52 years old, walking, working, and serving others, and the island breeze still blows down the narrow streets of Nassau.

My heart melted as Melanie shared this story with me. I knew of her dad and all he had done for his girls. But, hearing Melanie share the story really made me think. Her father left a legacy of value for not only one of his daughters but for both of them. To one he gave the gift of a better future, because he envisioned the possibilities in spite of the obstacles. To the other daughter, he gave the gift of love. His legacy as a father and as a leader continues to live on in the lives of two beautiful women who to this day envision the possibilities of a better tomorrow.

It's wonderful when you can look forward to something. In this case, becoming the person that you envision you can be. This is what my friend Kevin McCarthy, author of *The On-Purpose Person,* wants for us and why he has dedicated his leadership career to helping others be "on-purpose." Kevin shares a story about his encounter with a Valuable Leader. The story speaks to why knowing your purpose, what you were made for or what you were created to do, calls you to greater accomplishments.

Bob Bennett wasn't just any head tennis professional. He was a late-in-life entrepreneur living his dream. He had taken early retirement and owned and operated a four-court indoor tennis club in suburban Pittsburgh. Bob was a fine man who, in his younger years, had competed in national tennis tournaments. Bob was a leader with vision and he wove valuable leadership lessons into his hands-on training.

Kevin first met Bob in the summer of 1972, when Kevin was entering his senior year of high school. Bob's club was under construction back then and Kevin would regularly appear onsite at the membership trailer to pester Bob to give him a job. Eventually Bob gave in and hired Kevin to work the odd weekend hours at the reception desk. Through high school and even after his college years, Kevin worked in this family-owned business. Eventually, he became assistant tennis pro under Bob, and all those years he strung racquets, lots of racquets.

Kevin recalls his first time stringing a racquet: "As a competitive 17-year-old tennis player, I had never strung a tennis racquet before." On his first day on the job, Bob showed Kevin the ropes – perhaps the "strings" is the more descriptive term – about the fine art of transforming a tennis frame into a tennis racquet.

Bob and Kevin gathered around the stringing machine, an odd looking, chest-high contraption of metal, a calibrated weight, and moving parts. Bob handed Kevin an empty frame to mount on the stringing machine. Mounting the racquet was crucial to the integrity of the frame as each string was pulled with tension, clamped, and released. Bob checked Kevin's mount for a secure and proper fit, and looked at him as he smiled and nodded his approval.

Bob then handed Kevin a set of strings and had him count off seven racquet lengths for the main strings. With a pair of wire cutters, Kevin made the cut that created the main and the cross strings. Grasping the main string length, Bob had Kevin thread each end of the string into the top two center holes of the frame and pull each through a corresponding hole at the bottom of the frame. Holding the ends in each hand, Kevin would walk as far as the string would go, even the ends, drop them, and walk back to the stringer. He clamped the main string on the right and tensioned the string on the left. Then Bob inspected his work and once again grinned his approval.

Once the main strings were in place, the cross strings had to be woven into place. Bob showed Kevin various techniques to avoid "burning" the main strings from friction. Finally, the cross strings were in place and the last knot tied, and the time had come to dismount the racquet from the stringer, straighten any crooked strings, and then clip any excess strings.

Viola! His first racquet was complete! Bob inspected the racquet with a serious look as he carefully examined the frame. Bob then flipped the racquet in his right hand, hit his left hand with the string bed and declared, "Kevin, very well done!"

Kevin was delighted with his accomplishment and Bob's nod of approval, but Bob wasted no time and snatched another racquet from the workbench. "Here, do the same thing with this one," Bob said, and left the club. To Kevin's amazement, he was left to fly solo on his next one.

Striding into the club an hour later as promised, Bob asked, "Kevin, how's it going?" Kevin handed him a freshly strung racquet and, after inspecting the racquet, Bob declared, "Like I thought, you're a natural. Great work, young man!" Bob knew exactly what he was doing. He watched Kevin and his eagerness and envisioned what he could do.

Decades later Kevin still draws on his first string job when he's training others. Bob installed confidence into his life. Bob mentored and encouraged him. Bob trusted him and allowed him the opportunity to succeed or "fail forward" on his own. Most of all, Bob cast a vision for Kevin. You could say Bob envisioned who Kevin could become.

These stories both illustrate the second step on the journey to becoming a Valuable Leader: envision the future. As leaders we have to envision the opportunities and possibilities, turn obstacles into opportunities, and seek the wisdom of our team and others, both inside and outside our organizations. A valuable quality of a leader is demonstrated when the leader is willing to transfer power to others, based on his or her vision, to get the job done. As leaders we know that planning is easier when everyone on your team agrees on the final destination. We need to see the end state and communicate what we see to our teams so everyone knows where we are headed.

Here are three practical ways to begin the process of envisioning your possibilities:

1. Close your eyes and envision what you will accomplish in the next year or two.

2. Get input from all team members – what do they think the team can accomplish?

3. Communicate that plan to all members of the team.

Let's take the next step. Please come along.

Clearer Vision.

Perhaps you are a new leader or have been a leader for a long time. Now what's next?

Build your clear path forward. Sharpen your ability to envision your potential to be a more Valuable Leader. Be the leader who others want to follow, not have to. Learn more about the value of leading with vision by watching my video series.

Visit **TheValuableLeader.com**.

CHAPTER 3. TAKE ACTION: FOLLOW YOUR INSTINCTS, GO WITH YOUR GUT

"The most difficult thing is the decision to act, the rest is merely tenacity."

— Amelia Earhart

NOTHING HAPPENS UNTIL SOMEONE TAKES ACTION. Action takes energy, and, interestingly enough, when you read about successful leaders, you learn that one major trait they all have in common is they take action. They take action with the intent to make a difference either in their lives, or the lives of others. The saying that actions speak louder than words is also relevant for the Valuable Leader. The definition of action is "something that a person or group does; things done to achieve a particular purpose."

The third step on your path to becoming *the Valuable Leader* is to take ACTION. Valuable leaders *act*.

When we are given the title of leader, the title comes with the responsibility of making things happen. However, we all know of people in positions of leadership, yet we question their leadership value. Why? Because we all come to expect that leaders should be the ones out in front. They should be giving direction and taking action for others to follow. While you don't have to do the job on your own as a leader – in fact, great leaders never do – you must still make the first move.

My challenge to you is to position yourself as a leader who values action by being a leader who takes action!

Did you grow up thinking, "I want to be a follower someday"? Probably not. I did not either. I remember as a child, I would play a game called "follow the leader." As a youngster, I played follow the leader, but somehow I never wanted to grow up and be a follower. I wanted to follow the leader to learn what leaders do so that I could one day be the leader. *The Valuable Leader* focuses on charting the course and providing others the opportunity to engage and take action immediately. People learn by example. Your people should work with you, not just for you. They should see how the value of you taking action makes a difference for others: a difference that carries a lasting, positive impact.

I believe that a leader who values action is one who is focused on results. A leader understands that sometimes you will fail, but you learn from your failures. You "fail forward." Leaders know that standing still is not acceptable, but neither is deflecting the decision to go or not go onto the shoulders of others. Yes, you empower others to lead and take action, but a leader uses the art of delegation, not dumping. The buck, as they say, stops with the leader. A leader who values action knows the value of empowerment. When a leader empowers others, the leader endows them with the authority to take action and supports them along the way. But, while the leader transfers the authority, that leader knows that the ultimate responsibility of any action sits on his or her shoulders. True leaders are accountable.

Setting priorities is fundamental to leading others to action because all things cannot be done all at once. Wisdom in leadership is action with accountability. Begin, as Dr. Stephen Covey says, "with the end in mind." Put your vision into action; share your values with others, harvest their thoughts and ideas, and create a plan forward – together.

In addition to a focus on getting things

done and setting priorities, a great leader becomes a Valuable Leader when he or she moves beyond tasks to people. There have been many lessons learned about the people side of leadership, but I believe that we all become valuable leaders who take action when we focus on three key things:

Communicating openly

Building trust

Being authentic

Communicating openly means to listen as well as to speak. With so much technology available today, we need to remember the value of taking action with face-to-face communication. This takes time, but the results are invaluable because in-person communication sets the foundation for a strong and Valuable Leader. Listening to what others are saying lets them know they are valued. Morale is boosted and so is employee engagement.

Building trust is a result of open communication. Once we get to know people by investing time to listen and speak with them, we take actions that result in trust. Trust cannot be demanded or controlled. Trust is something leaders must earn. Additionally, if employees feel they cannot trust their leader, then engagement, commitment, and performance all suffer. Building trust through action shows the team that its leader is about showing versus telling. The importance of communicating openly cannot be overstated!

The old proverb is true: Actions *do* speak louder than words.

Finally, being authentic is a simple action leaders can take daily, yet the trait of authenticity is seen as one of the most difficult. So many leaders are afraid of being themselves, because they feel they must have an image, a certain "leadership" image that they must portray. Nonsense! People want to do business with real people. People want to do business with people they can trust.

To be authentic is first to be true to you. You cannot be a Valuable Leader when you don't value yourself by being who you really are. This is fundamental and also complex.

So, if I had to say what was the key component in my decision to value action, I would say that you should take action by demonstrating your ability to communicate openly, by building trust at the individual level, and by being yourself – the real you. Being who you really are is the best action you can take and the greatest reward you will receive.

How many times have we said to ourselves, "I have this to do and that to do," but we don't get the task done? How many of you would say that you are great at planning, but struggle with procrastination, with actually getting things done? You find making a list of tasks to do tomorrow is easy, but many times you find that "tomorrow" never comes.

I love the saying, "Some people make things happen, and others wonder what happened?" The value of action is that results matter. Productivity is the name of the game. In my "Kick Procrastination into Productivity" workshop, I teach a simple five-step strategy to taking action. Why? Because I have a tendency to procrastinate myself; maybe you do, too.

I have learned that successful leaders try many different approaches until they find the one that works. People often look at leaders and wonder how and why they are so successful. They are so because, in a large part, they simply chose to take action. Mark Twain said:

"Eighty percent of life is simply showing up!"

I would add to Twain's statement and say that nothing happens until we take action. Tomorrow's growth starts today.

You might recall earlier in the book that I came from the Bahamas to the U.S. to begin college. This step to enroll in college was a result of numerous deliberate actions. My enrollment came after awareness on my part that there was tremendous value in having a higher education.

The first step in anything is to be aware of your need. Once we recognize we have a need, we can then decide if we want to do something about meeting that need. I became aware of my need for growth in the early 1980s. I had just completed my high school education and jumped into my first full-time job as an office assistant for The Bahamas National Trust. The purpose of The Bahamas National Trust was to raise awareness of the need for environmental protection to preserve the islands for future generations. This noble cause increased my awareness of my need to grow. I had to take action to move from where I was to where I wanted to be.

I was following the path that so many of my loved ones had taken before me, which was to graduate from high school, get a job, take care of your family, get married, and then get a better job to take even better care of your family.

Not long into my job at The Trust, my need to grow became very apparent. I did not understand the need then, but I do now: I wanted to live "The Law of the Rubber Band." John Maxwell writes in his book, *The 15 Invaluable Laws of Growth:*

"Growth stops when you lose the tension between where you are and where you could be."

I realized that if I stayed where I was, if I did not take the risk of investing in my growth, I would not achieve the dreams that I had deep inside of me. I knew there was a different path for me. This desire for growth challenged me to take the road less traveled. Where did that road take me? How did I grow?

I came to the realization, over the next two years, that higher education was the key to my future. Pursuing a higher education would enable me to better realize my vision of being a more valuable person. I could give myself greater value and, although I did not realize the benefit then, I could pass value on to others too. Going to college and choosing a field to study would be the catalyst for my growth. The common thread that all of the people working around me had experienced was the achievement of higher education. I needed to pursue more challenging educational goals if I wanted to grow.

The acclaimed Rabbi Nachman of Bratslav, the founder of the Breslov Hasidic movement, stated:

"If you won't be better tomorrow than you were today, then what do you need tomorrow for?"

The leaders of The Trust knew they needed to stretch themselves to preserve the environment for subsequent generations. Since The Trust was a not-for-profit and needed funding to accomplish its goals, a Heritage Fund was created to sustain the day-to-day operations. The Trust hired an expert in professional fundraising, and I worked with the team that raised $3 million over the course of three years.

People took action and gave money to help protect the environment because they wanted to make a positive difference for the future. People cared and took action. Gradually it dawned on me that; "Perhaps there are people who would be willing to make a difference for me. Perhaps there are people willing to take action to support my goal of a higher education. Would these same people be willing to help make my future better than today by funding my higher education?"

I decided to share what The Trust had done and how I thought I could use that same method with my mom. Allow me to share my story of taking action.

I came home from work at The Trust and told my mom the exciting news. "Mom, The Trust got a $1 million donation to its fundraising campaign today. Can you believe it? Mom, that got me thinking, maybe people would give me money to pay for my college education."

My mom turned, looked at me, and said,

in her Bahamian island accent, "Girl, are you are out of your mind? Nobody is going to give you a bunch of money just for you to go to school."

Tears welled up in my eyes and I ran out of the room. I really believed that I could work a program like The Trust did and raise money for my college education. Wiping the tears from my cheeks, I made a decision that day, a decision to take action. I made a list of prospects and started writing letters. I asked myself "Who *could* give me money? Who *would* give me money?"

With hope in my heart, I began my journey, first gaining acceptance to Webber International University. With my college acceptance letter in hand, all I needed was the money to cover my tuition and expenses. One week later I had my first appointment with a local attorney, Mr. Geoffrey Johnstone. I entered his office, confidently handed him my fundraising letter, sat down across from his big mahogany desk, and said, "Sir, I would like to invite you to help me pay for my college education. Can I count on you to sponsor me for one full year of college?"

Mr. Johnstone slowly and carefully read my letter. Then he looked up over his silver-rimmed reading glasses and said, "Yes, I will help you, and, if your grades are good, come back and see me again." That day I left his office with my first check towards college! Looking back, I think maybe he believed in me more than I believed in myself.

Over the next 12 months there were more than 20 appointments, and over 50 letters sent out. I diligently worked the professional fundraising principles I had learned at The Trust and raised over $100,000. Not only were these funds sufficient to cover the cost of my undergraduate degree, they would also cover the cost of my graduate degree! I was on my way to college. Were there people who told me no? Of course, but there were enough people who said yes! The people who took action for the nonprofit also took action to help me.

Fast forward to the day I started at college. As my sister, my mom and I drove up to the campus of Webber International University in Babson Park, Florida, this time the tears were in my mom's eyes. She was smiling at me and confidently said in her best Bahamian accent, "Baby, mummy is so proud of you."

Friends, my fundraising story taught me a valuable lesson. There will always be naysayers. People will tell you no, and success won't come easy. But, in the end, you will succeed, not because of luck or happenstance, but because you made the choice to be a leader and take action!

As I reflect, I know my success was because leaders like Geoffrey Johnstone took action, made a difference, and pivoted my life onto a new path. Yes, my willingness to stretch myself "outside my comfort zone" enabled me to succeed. However, the tenderhearted people, the leaders who said, "Yes, I will help you," and then took action to do so, made the greatest impact. Today my life is one centered on living "The Law of the Rubber Band." The Law that states: To accomplish a better tomorrow, I know I ought to do something challenging today. I must take action and value the action taken by others!

What are you doing today that will propel you into a better tomorrow? What are you doing today to make a difference for others? These are the tough questions that require leaders to make a decision. Do they take action themselves or pass that decision on to another person, someone else who can lead?

My hope is that you are challenged by my story to stretch yourself, challenged to grow yourself, to move forward, take action, and achieve your dreams. Friend, your better tomorrow starts today.

When I thought of action by others, my friend Yolanda Torres Cox, a Valuable Leader in her own right, came to mind. I had the pleasure of serving on a team where she was our leader. Yolanda has a servant's heart and she backs up her service by being a woman who is not afraid to take action. We could be in the middle of a crowd and a lady accidentally spills coffee and Yolanda will be the one to spring into action and run to clean up the mess. Yolanda knows all about taking action and, of course, when I invited her to share a story, she did not hesitate. She shares this story of her father, Miguel Torres.

Yolanda says, "We are so much alike it's crazy."

Her father was a man who believed in taking action. He pressed others to take action as well and not simply sit on the sidelines. Growing up as the only girl in the home with two older brothers, Yolanda learned to always stand up for herself, stand up for others, and for what was right. She remarks, "It's funny to think how much I appreciate my father's discipline and example in my life today, because I felt he was way too hard on me when I was growing up."

Her mind goes back to the time when she was eight years old, to the time she first learned to ride a bike without training wheels. Yolanda remembers her father putting the bike together and telling her to hop on the bike. She was really afraid to ride. With a stern but loving look, Miguel persuaded her to get on her bike. In her mind, Yolanda knew she had to have strength much the same way her father did – there was no doubt – she was going to ride that bike without training wheels! Oh and by the way, there was no room for complaining either. She sat on the bike, took off, and ran right into the fence! That was enough of taking action right? Wrong! Her father didn't let her stop after that first try. He wanted her to keep trying to ride over and over again until she got the hang of it. What he really wanted was for her not to be afraid to take action, even if she failed the first time. He wanted her to get up and try to ride that bike, time and again, until she succeeded.

Miguel knew that children enjoy bike riding and he did not want his only daughter to miss out on the joys of this experience.

Yolanda also remembers a time when she went to get her first car. She was so frustrated because, unlike her brother, who had multiple cars given to him, she had to save up the money and buy her own car. Yolanda recalls she could only afford a beat-up Saturn, a manual shift with a bad alternator to boot! She and her father went to the junkyard to purchase a "new" alternator. No, they didn't take the car to a mechanic; Miguel wanted her to install the alternator herself. He walked her through the steps, guiding her all the time, but he wanted Yolanda to take action. He wanted her to be the leader to fix the car. She began to install the alternator, fighting, kicking, and screaming the whole time. She remembers looking up from under the hood when her father looked at her and remarked, "You know I'm teaching you to be independent, to do things for yourself, right? Never quit."

Those two little words have stuck with Yolanda since then and taught her to be a woman of action, "to go for it." To never quit! When times are hard, or things don't go her way, she always remembers her dad's advice, to be a woman of action and "never quit." This advice would serve Yolanda well as she sought to live her dream of joining the police academy and becoming a detective. Yolanda applied and was denied twice. But she did not give up. She continued to apply as she recalled her past experiences and heard her father say: "Keep trying.

Never quit." The voice of her father still remains in the forefront of her mind.

Today Yolanda continues to take action as a detective for the local police department. She has learned that people of action don't sit on the sidelines. She has learned that when you continue "to go for it" and take action, then you can achieve your full potential. At times things will be difficult, but you must persevere, continue to act, and move forward. When Yolanda looks back on all those tough times, she says, "I'm thankful for that stubborn old man. If it weren't for him, I don't think that I would be nearly as fierce and caring of a leader as I am today."

Being a leader is not always glorious. In fact, being a leader can be tough. Sometimes you have to apply what most of us have experienced, but perhaps few of us have applied to ourselves: tough love. That's what Miguel was doing for his daughter. As leaders, this is exactly what we must do to help others reach their full potential; we must refuse to give up on others so they learn not to give up on themselves. When we become a Valuable Leader we understand our real value and others appreciate our real worth.

I would like to share another story from

a friend I met at Bayside Community Church. My friend Rob Smith is a jack-of-all-trades. Since I have known Rob in the last two years, he has eagerly embraced positions from leading auditorium setup, to leading hospitality services, to working part time at the church. In addition to all of this, Rob is a dedicated father to his four children and a loving husband to his wife, Brenna.

Rob is always seeking to get things done, not just completed, but done the right way. I wondered what the origin of Rob's action-oriented style was. Rob shared this story about one of the leaders in his life. I think Rob's story brings clarity to the source of his own style, and represents a good example of a leader who takes action.

Rob had a mentor, Dave Murray, who held a leadership position as an executive pastor at a church where he served a few years ago. His pastor did not lean on his title or position; rather, he felt to be a man who took action was more important. Through his action, a trait lived out by a Valuable Leader, Pastor Dave was able to influence his people.

Rob recalls his pastor first seeking to have a vision. By inviting stakeholders to assist in the development and implementation of a vision framework, Pastor Dave was actively working to build organizational alignment.

Rob's pastor was also not afraid to step out and make a decision, to take a risk. He would help both men and women, offering them valuable work experience and a sense of self-worth. Whether the person had prior experience for the job did not matter. Pastor Dave would provide each of them with a clear outline of the responsibilities in his or her new role. By also holding them accountable, they learned responsibility for their actions. Rob's pastor created a healthy and enjoyable work environment.

Providing clarity and understanding was also important to Pastor Dave. He always sought to listen before he took action, because he felt that getting clarity on the situation was important before acting. He understood that people did not always agree. Rob notes that because of Pastor Dave's leadership, he learned that acting with wisdom was more important than making a popular decision.

Rob recalls goals being set each year. At times, based on feedback the pastor had received from his members and monitoring their activities, changes would be necessary. Pastor Dave was not afraid to adjust the course, to take action and change direction, to achieve the desired results.

Pastor Dave was more a leader than simply a steward or a manager. He carefully observed and listened to each member. He sought to see each person grow and become the best they could be. At times when there came a need for an individual to transition into a role that was a better fit, Pastor Dave would work with that person to find a platform that was better suited for his or her talents, gifts, and abilities. This could often mean taking chances on people, but he was a man of action, unafraid to step out and "adjust the sails," so to speak.

Rob credits much of his impact as a leader to the time spent with Pastor Dave. The lessons Rob learned during those years have helped him grow into the leader he is today.

Are you a leader who takes action? What action do you need to take *today* to move you forward tomorrow in the direction to be a Valuable Leader?

Taking action is the difference between making things happen and wondering what happened.

As leaders, our responsibility is to make things happen for the better. Begin today with this simple three-step process. On your piece of paper or on the Notes page in the back of this book, write your answers to the following questions:

1.   What is your action plan to focus on advancing the goals for you and your team? List two things you will accomplish within the next two weeks for yourself and each of your employees.

2.   Begin to set priorities: who must do what and by when?

3.   How will you inspect what you expect? Set your team up for success with regular check-ins on each member's progress.

It's time for action. Take your next step.

Inspired?
Ready for Action?

Take your first step. Act now! Be a leader who takes action.

Take a peek at my video series. Learn more about the workshops I conduct to help you kick procrastination into productivity.

Find out more at **TheValuableLeader.com**.

CHAPTER 4. DEVELOP: FOLLOW THE SCENT OF GROWTH

"The growth and development of people is the highest calling of leadership."

— Harvey S. Firestone

WHEN YOU ARE A LEADER YOUR FOCUS IS LESS ABOUT YOU AND MORE ABOUT OTHERS. Leaders know the reason they lead is because they have people willing to follow them.

No one grows up dreaming to be a follower; people grow up dreaming about being a leader. A leader's responsibility is to develop leaders, not followers. To develop is "to cause something or someone to grow or become bigger or more advanced."

The fourth step on your path to

becoming a Valuable Leader is to DEVELOP yourself and others. Valuable leaders *grow!*

For leaders to lead, they must influence others. But how do you influence others? You influence others when you get them to want to follow you. Without followers, you are not a leader. You are only leading one person – yourself. As the song goes, one is the loneliest number. While we all start out as leaders first leading ourselves, our ability to lead and add value opens the door to our opportunity to lead others. We move from leading projects and tasks and things to the higher purpose of leading people to accomplish great things collectively.

Have you been leading people or things? Someone once said people don't leave companies; people leave their managers. I would say "managers" because great leaders don't lose employees to other leaders or companies. Great leaders know that their people are both the reason for and a happy consequence of their success. When leaders learn the value of developing others, they themselves become better leaders, and create loyal leaders who follow them for life.

Valuable leaders don't hold their employees back. They encourage their employees to seek growth opportunities, even if those opportunities are at other companies or in other departments. In fact, great leaders who understand the value of leading will work their team members out of a job so that they can be promoted into other growth opportunities. Truly valuable leaders value others so much that they give them away for greater growth.

What a leader does to impact the growth of his or her people is the characteristic that sets valuable leaders apart. You know when you have found a Valuable Leader because you see how that person is followed. Valuable leaders invest in their people. Valuable leaders are not so much about what they can get out of their employees and others, but much more about whom they can mentor and stretch to reach their full potential. We should all strive to become a leader who creates other leaders. This is what we mean when we say become a Valuable Leader!

Giving your time as a leader to ensure every employee has a growth plan shows that leadership is about advancement. Valuable leaders focus on the potential of their employees, knowing that each individual is unique. Encouraging your team to fully leverage its strengths demonstrates that you are a leader who sees value in developing and then marshaling each team member's core competencies. Recognition of the immense value of diversity and inclusion is regarded as an essential quality of a Valuable Leader today.

So much has been written in the last decade about diversity in the workforce, but blind spots still remain around this topic in leadership. There are no one-size-fits-all leaders. However, great leaders go beyond respecting diversity: they seek out how to strengthen the whole team by individually valuing the potential that comes from diversity. People all grow and improve through a wide set of experiences and backgrounds. Today's leaders have to adopt a value-based perspective when leading others. People don't only want to do a job; they want leaders who value their thinking, their strengths and humanity, and their potential.

In the development of others, leaders know that they must also be advancing themselves. Remember when I said, "You can't give what you don't have"? To value the growth of others means that the leader has learned to value his or her own growth. Recruiting value in your leadership will help you create a legacy that lasts a lifetime.

The challenge facing today's leader is how to develop others when generational mindsets have shifted from long-term employee tenure to the millennial, generation X's and Z's who tend to seek shorter-term career advancement. Loyalty, which was once highly prized and rewarded, has recently been replaced with a desire to stay with a company for approximately two years. Gone are the days when employees remained with a company for 20-plus years or more. Perhaps faithfulness in the workforce is being redefined. Perhaps loyalty is no longer about time – the years of employment – but more about the impact from your employment.

People development takes time. One school of thought is that if employees are not staying long with any one company, with shorter career spans, perhaps there is not time to invest in their development. Investing the time – regardless of the length of time – will differentiate a good leader from a great leader, one who is truly valuable.

I have come to believe that development of a leader who is valued does not come with a time limit. All leaders have the responsibility to invest in their own growth and that of the people they lead. Growth is an ongoing process. You don't only grow once and then you're done. The growth of leaders, of every one of us, for that matter, is not an option: continuous growth is a must-do. People development is hard work. Leaders who invest in themselves and their people reap the great benefits of personal and professional growth. When you discover your real value companies will reward you for your real worth.

Building a Valuable Leader mindset advances the whole organization. No one grows from doing the same thing over and over again. Valuable leaders stretch themselves and their teams. Through coaching, mentoring, and professional training, new skills are created, new ideas are born, and new leaders arise.

Mother Teresa, an entrepreneur, nun, and missionary, was a woman who saw a need for the development of others. In 1950, Mother Teresa established The Missionaries of Charity, which was built to help the less fortunate people of society with both physical and spiritual needs. The Missionaries of Charity reached over 4,000 members under her leadership and served over 25 countries across five continents.

In 1979, Mother Teresa was awarded the Nobel Peace Prize because she did a tremendous amount of work to influence others who, in return, bridged the gap of a suffering society. Today, her work still influences others and is making real, valuable change in the lives of so many underprivileged people.

I am sure you would agree that Mother Teresa was a leader. Even if we might not agree with all her views, we can all agree that she influenced others, that she was someone who wanted to help develop others and give them an opportunity for a better life. We must be able to influence others who come alongside us and support or follow our vision. Without that skill we may be unable to lead others. Mother Teresa knew and lived a life that valued others through influence.

While I never met Mother Teresa, I have been very blessed to come to know a woman who I would say exhibits the qualities portrayed by her. I guess you could say I got to know my very own "Mother Teresa."

Here is my modern-day story of a similar woman, a story that is personal to me, and is about someone you have probably never heard of. Her name is Joy Rampello.

In 1990 I came to know Joy, first as my Sunday school teacher and then as my treasured friend. When I met Joy, she was in her mid 60s, a retired biology schoolteacher, a homemaker, beloved wife, a devoted mother, and faithful Christian. And, oh yes, there's more. She was a passionate bird watcher.

Earlier in our journey I told you that we would take a deeper dive into my passion for bird watching, so here's where I left off. I did not watch birds before I met Joy, but she did not take long to convince me that I should. One day while we were walking in a local nature park, Joy began to point out the different birds. "There he goes," she said, as we both caught a glimpse of a little Northern Parula, a small songbird about the size of your thumb. She would gasp and say, "Oh my! How beautiful is that tiny little feathered one? God is such an amazing Creator, isn't he,

Veli?" ("Veli" is my nickname.)

Her passion was contagious.

To my own surprise, I began to feel the passion she felt as I looked closer and closer at the birds. I heard myself saying, "Wow, that little bird is so precious." Then there was another one and another one. Before I knew what was happening, I was hooked. I was an official bird nerd; all because Joy had influenced me to look closer.

Since 1990, Joy's influence has caused me to develop a deep appreciation for birds, so much so that I have travelled all across the U.S., Canada, and the Caribbean, even going as far as Australia, to see over twelve hundred species of birds. All for the rapture of watching birds. My friend Joy influenced me so much. I not only watch birds but I have also captured them in over 50,000 photographs. I've written stories about birds and yes, have even had the honor of having my articles and photographs published in a few major magazines.

I tell you this story of Joy and how she influenced me not to get you to look at birds or to scare you into thinking you could become a bird nerd like I am. I share this story with you to illustrate that like the story of Mother Teresa, the proof of leadership is when you can see how you are developing and influencing others to follow your vision and seek to know more: To grow and develop oneself. That's what Joy's leadership did. She influenced and encouraged me to grow, all through her passion for birds.

Who would have thought that birds would be something that would expand my thinking, my experiences, and my life? My walk with Joy has taken me on a fantastic journey, to a whole new level of appreciation for my Creator and His creations. Like Mother Teresa, my friend, Joy, has learned the secret to leadership. And that secret is "to become a Valuable Leader."

Our ability to influence others, to lead others, to help others grow, might come in ways we would not have normally expected. Joy has never been an entrepreneur nor won the Nobel Peace Prize, and she would never agree with me that she is a leader. But, I hope that you take a closer look at leadership and see that like Joy you too can influence others. You can influence others and help them to grow.

Do you have a Joy or Mother Teresa in your life? Is there a Valuable Leader who has influenced you to be a better leader, in your life and business? Or are you, perhaps, that Valuable Leader to someone else? These are the questions that I would challenge you to consider.

Stretching ourselves always requires us to change. There are people who have the mindset that they don't need to grow. We say to ourselves; "I have my job, I'm content. Why rock the boat?" But, leaders know the power of growth and influence. Dale Galloway, author of 22 books, a pastor, and teacher says:

"The growth and development of people is the highest calling of a leader."

How true! If you want to know how well you are doing as a leader, ask how much value you are adding to the lives of others. Look at the people you lead and you will see!

Growth does not simply "happen." We must be intentional. All great leaders invest themselves in a personal growth plan. Ask yourself: would you say that you have a personal growth plan? Do you have a plan for your leadership growth? How about a personal development plan for those you lead?

This book is your guide to your very own leadership development growth plan. But only reading this book without taking action will not move you forward. *The Valuable Leader* gives you seven steps that you can take to build your value. This book gives you real examples of real leaders who added real value to others. Their lives are mirrors that we can look into and see all that we do, too. Knowing the steps without taking action on them will not move you forward. Remember, your tomorrow's growth must start today.

One way to help with your growth plan is to read books and take courses, like you are doing here. Another way is to get a coach. We all need a coach, even football stars and professional singers. You name the occupation or passion or profession. If a person wants to move from good to great, that person must have a coach. How about you? What will you do now that you are on this path, and becoming more aware than ever of what is essential to transform you into a Valuable Leader? When will you move toward increasing your value – move from good to great, from great to valuable, and from valuable to maybe even invaluable?

There is no time like the present to begin making the difference you deserve. I want this so much for you because I know that there are people who need your help, who need your leadership, and who need to know that there is a Valuable Leader out there waiting to meet them, listen to them, and develop them.

Consider a rubber band. In fact, stop reading and go take action. Go and get a rubber band and then come back to this page. Let's do a little virtual exercise together. I'll wait for you.

With your rubber band in hand, pull the band with a nice stretch. With both hands, pull both sides of the rubber band as far apart as you can. Let the band go back to the original size. Much like the rubber band in our little exercise, when we apply tension to and stretch ourselves, we see that we do not go back to our original capacity. We need to apply tension in our lives to move us from where we are to where we could be.

Stretching ourselves allows us to grow. To do more, be more, and achieve more. At each step of the way we must also take the time to celebrate where we are on our path to encourage the desire for future growth. I have heard, "motivation will get you going, but it will take discipline to keep you learning and growing."

For me, growth came when I took a closer look at my leadership.

In his book *How to Win Friends and Influence People,* Dale Carnegie, the well-known writer, lecturer, and developer of famous courses in topics from self-improvement to interpersonal skills, said this about influence:

"The only way on earth to influence the other fellow is to talk about what he wants and show him how to get it."

Helping others achieve their dreams can be like a boomerang. The benefits will come back to you in ways that you never expected, ways that help you achieve your dreams. Why? Because for leaders to lead they must influence others. When you focus on others, you help them achieve their success. When we help others achieve their dreams and grow, we in turn will grow. You can't do something without the benefit of learning from your actions. I believe that successful leaders influence others to grow.

Unfortunately, most of the regrets people have in their lives are not a result of something they did, but normally come as a result of something they never did. Improving yourself is the best way to help yourself find your real value and help others. You cannot give what you do not have, and your ability to lead will only go as far as your growth allows. The more you grow, the more you will be able to enhance your leadership value and expand your influence. Like in our example of the rubber band, when you grow you never go back to your original self. You have more of yourself to offer.

However, you must value growth above and beyond yourself – beyond the way you are today. Your team needs to grow. In fact, I would propose that all leaders have the responsibility to value growth so much that they refuse to allow their teams and themselves to remain where they are. The status quo is the valuable leader's enemy.

The growth of a leader impacts individuals outside of business too. Leadership is all around us, if only we take the time to take a closer look.

This reminds me of another familiar story, a story about a mother who was a leader in her own right. A woman who knew that the value of a leader was in the life she lived.

Stella Pinder, a very dear friend of my family for many years, told me a story about her mother, Dale Darville. I would like to share her story with you. The story provides an example of a woman who valued the idea of growing and developing people.

Dale, or "Mum" as her girls fondly called her, was born in England, and was an only child. At the age of 11, she was sent off to boarding school and had to pretty much fend for herself, an experience that molded Dale into the woman she grew to be: a woman who was smart, independent, and had a strong desire to develop others. Dale married at a very young age and had two daughters: Stella and her sister Diana. Shortly after having both children she decided to move the family to the Bahamas. Dale needed the warmer, more suitable climate of the Bahamas, so she made the move with only her two girls and herself.

Despite the challenges in her young life, Stella recalls: "My Mum was always a positive person, looking for the good in everyone and every situation.

She fell in love with a handsome Bahamian gentleman named Michael Darville. He not only fell in love with my mum, but also with my sister and me. He loved our whole family."

Stella goes on to say, "You could say that my Mum's profession was first and foremost being a wonderful mother, wife, and homemaker. She took on a part-time job in a shop where she sold local woodcarvings. Mum would take time to paint beautiful scenes of Bahamian sunsets and seascapes on the paper bags she used to hold the customers' purchases. She wanted them to love the islands as much as she did." The customers all loved that personal touch, and they would often return on their next visit.

Stella remembers how Dale was a member of several charitable organizations. Dale loved fundraising events that were focused on caring for and nurturing less fortunate children. Stella describes a typical holiday season: "At Christmas I would wrap dozens of gifts with Mum and then head over to the Children's Emergency Hostel." Dale knew the importance of investing in children, no matter what their age or situation. Dale knew that teaching her girls the importance of giving back and spending time would help them and the hostel children develop into strong leaders with kind hearts. The hostel children loved Dale so much they would call her the "fairy godmother."

Dale showed leadership in her handling of daily life. She was extremely generous and kind and could not do enough for others. Her heart's desire was for others, especially children, to have opportunities to learn and grow. That's why she invested so much time with the children, including her own. Having their faces light up with joy because they learned something new, that was the reward most precious to Dale and Dale was the most precious reward to those children.

I had the pleasure of knowing Stella's mum – "Mrs. D.," as I affectionately called her. She was a woman with the sweetest smile. I am pretty sure if you looked up the word "gentleness" in the dictionary, you would find a picture of Mrs. D. there. I was a young kid myself when I met her, and I know, personally, how much she valued the importance of helping others grow. Mrs. D. would let me visit her home on Sunday afternoons and play board games. She made me feel special and valued as an individual, even though I was kid among a number of adults, and for that I will be forever grateful.

The second story I would like to share with you is short and very meaningful. The story comes from one of the leaders I had the privilege of working with early in my career. His name is John Counter. John is a man of faith and strong character. He is a man for whom I have great admiration: a man who played an important part in showing me the qualities of a Valuable Leader. I am honored to call John my mentor, my friend, my Valuable Leader.

When I asked John to contribute his story to the book, he did not hesitate. As he pondered the task of defining what a Valuable Leader was, he decided to look back and share how he had evolved as a leader from his personal life experiences. He felt persuaded to establish certain parameters that would help with the scope of this task.

John's first thought was of those in his life who he believed were leaders who influenced him and contributed to his growth. Those leaders who helped shape him into the wonderful leader he became in life. John recalls a time when he was a kid growing up in a small town.

His dad, the leader of their home, made such a powerful impact on him. John credits his dad with being the role model of his life. John recalls: "I felt my dad could do everything well and provided the security I needed growing up." Then there was the lifeguard at the lake who, although John could hardly walk, taught him how to swim, and not to be afraid of the water. To a young child, this was a big deal!

As time passed, there were other leaders of increasing significance in John's life. Throughout grammar school, junior high, and high school, John had a broad range of teachers who contributed to his advancement. There were teachers who were outstanding as leaders and they influenced his life's direction in terms of career aspirations and opportunities.

At a critical age, there was the Boy Scout experience with leaders who taught him ways to become self-sufficient in thought, in word, and in deeds. These leaders invested in John through their caring leadership and training at the scout house and weekend camping trips. John learned valuable survival skills that benefited him throughout his life.

There were many other leaders who impacted John. Leaders in church, college, military, family, friends, neighbors, and the benefit of a 50-year working career, all provided an increased level of influence on his life, his maturity, and his leadership skillset.

What was the conclusion that John came to after considering all the leaders who both shaped and influenced his life? Well, the first conclusion was that teachers are not necessarily leaders. However, leaders are always teachers. Leaders always take time to nurture people. The second point was that leaders also influence others to be leaders. Finally, through his life experiences, John is convinced that there were leaders who had pure motives and influenced him in positive ways. Other leaders had selfish motives and were disappointing over time.

John's story reminded me that there are many leaders who enter our lives and, while there are leaders who help us to grow from positive experiences, there are other leaders who, unfortunately, help us to grow from disappointing experiences. There is no manual for leadership success. The success of your leadership impact comes from the lessons you learn in life. Great leaders seek to be better leaders today than they were yesterday and strive to be even better leaders tomorrow.

My time spent working with John,

although not long in years, was deep in value. He is a learning leader. I know why he added so much value to me and all my peers under his leadership. He values the importance of growth. I bet if I called John at this moment, he would be asking me: "What did you learn today?" He is that kind of Valuable Leader.

Now I will ask you: What did you learn today? What did you do to help someone else learn something that he or she did not know yesterday?

Developing people is a very important step on the path to becoming a Valuable Leader, but taking that step is not always easy. Perhaps you are already doing things to invest in others, to add value to their growth. Perhaps you are already doing this for yourself, too. Whether you are doing that at present or if you are ready to do so tomorrow, I want to encourage you to take action. Here are a few basic thoughts to get you started practicing in the development of yourself and others:

1. Pay it forward. You are indeed the leader you are today because people invested in you. Do the same for others. Write down the names of two people you can invest in to help them grow. Then begin by helping them to grow.

2. Stay on the cutting edge, so that you are in constant growth mode for the

benefit of yourself and your team. Commit to reading one personal development book in the subject areas of communication, change, or collaboration. Commit to reading more if you are ambitious.

3. Be okay with not knowing all the answers, but keep in mind that the answers lie within your team. Seek to understand.

Your growth continues with the next step. Let's keep moving forward.

Develop to Influence.

You cannot give what you do not have.

Invest in your development and grow your influence. Move from where you are and become a more valued leader. Learn the secrets to developing the leader in you in my exclusive video series. Watch now!

Go to **TheValuableLeader.com**.

CHAPTER 5. ENGAGE WITH OTHERS: LEAD WITH A HUMAN TOUCH

"Leaders create an environment of engagement where every employee says: 'I am valued.'"

— Velma Knowles

LEADERS WHO ARE THE MOST SUCCESSFUL GET THEIR EMPLOYEES INVOLVED. Real leaders engage their people. They understand the power of many versus the power of one. To engage is to do or take part in something.

The fifth step on your path to becoming a Valuable Leader is to ENGAGE. Valuable leaders *include* others.

One of the hottest topics in the business conversation today is "employee engagement." Companies are realizing excellent growth and formidable success with board and shareholder approval, while at the same time struggling with high employee turnover and low employee engagement. Why?

One thought is that the business can experience financial success and employee failure at the same time because management can increase profits through consolidation, synergies, cost cutting, and more. All of these completely impact the bottom line, but at the same time make no similar impact in engaging the employees.

Growth in profits will come at a price – for this is but a short-term success. Research confirms that disconnected and unengaged employees will cost a business more than it realizes in the areas of culture, morale, innovation, and leadership. Without employees who are engaged, ongoing business relevance, customer service and satisfaction, as well as brand value, future results, and foundation, will be crushed.

Herein lies the challenge for leaders. As a Valuable Leader you know the crucial importance of employee engagement and business sustainability. The good news for organizations that develop valuable leaders is that these leaders have the foresight and behaviors that will create a belief system where employees become engaged. To have your employees engaged you must start at the top. Your leaders must be engaged!

Engaging leaders get personal and provide guiding principles that steer the organizational ship. They seek out the gifts of everyone and get to know them beyond the employee-leader relationship. They know their employees as people: people with families, dreams, fears, and, yes, goals. For your organization to have a workforce of employees who are engaged, the company needs to be first and foremost engaged with its leaders. Shoulder to shoulder, you must lead from a position of the heart. Energize your staff members; give them purpose; appreciate them for their efforts; speak for them; value them for their real worth; and be authentic. When people see leaders as people and not the unapproachable "boss" in the corner office, they connect and want to become a part of the team.

The power of engagement needs to be part of the organizational culture. The beliefs of the leader and organization can create the atmosphere needed to engage others. Engagement is about communication, openhearted communication that instills trust. All leaders are in the business of human capital development. When organizations pull the entire workforce together, providing opportunity for growth and valuing individual contributions, only then will strategies project a culture that exhibits energy, excitement, and employee engagement.

As the leader in today's environment, you are the one called upon to lead engagement. You must be the change agent to engage. No one should be left behind. Your success is fundamentally a result of the success of your people. To best understand each employee's engagement, you must measure the existing level of engagement. This is the benchmark that enables you to track how and when you are making a positive impact.

While you must lead employee engagement, you cannot make people become engaged. Commitment to an organization is an individual choice. Leaders must create an organizational culture that fosters the value of people engagement. You must provide the "why" behind their question of "what's in it for me?" You need to be the role model for employee engagement by caring enough to take the lead on the following actions:

Walk in your employees' shoes

Lead yourself first and seek to engage with others

Create a clear purpose for individuals to

contribute

Encourage a learning culture for growth

Your greatest return will be the transformation of a company with a group of people to a company that is defined as a premier organization, positioned for success through the value of a talented team.

Leaders know there is power in teamwork. The ability of a leader to collectively get the team to work together is a valuable skill. The mark of a Valuable Leader is evident when that leader successfully engages his or her staff to move from a group of people to a high-performing team.

Valuable leaders understand the concept of SOAR: Strengths, Opportunities, Attitudes, and Results. SOAR is a framework that I developed when I was working with a cross-functional group of middle to senior executives in an association on a non-dues revenue plan. All leaders on the team had their own thoughts on how the plan should be developed, what the key drivers of success should be, and how much budget would be required to achieve our goals.

Every person on the team had good intentions, but not everyone was engaged, nor did each person agree on the priorities. Allowing each team member the opportunity to share ideas took an investment of time. The team only moved forward by getting all the perspectives on the table and seeing the power in what members could do together. Individually, our growth would not achieve the goal, but collectively, engaged on the right priorities, we knew that our team could SOAR.

We drew from the strengths of each leader, knowing that we were better when we operated from our individual strengths. We quantified the opportunities, setting priorities based on the greatest reward and least amount of risk. We agreed to agree and to disagree, but do so with respect. Our attitude was one of professionalism and one based on key values of integrity, respect, and service. And, finally, we set key performance indicators to measure our results and adjust where needed. We learned the power of valuing each other and to SOAR through the value of engagement.

Our success was possible because the entire organization had a culture built on strong values. Leaders set the tone for the company's culture, and we knew that culture and performance are directly connected.

When we tap into the strengths of our teams, we can turn obstacles into opportunities. When we encourage a positive attitude within our organization, we help our teams focus on achieving sustainable results.

Everyone wants to be on a winning team. Your team members are no different. Set them up for success; engage them and they will SOAR.

Back in 2014, I was hired as a consultant to a large association. There were 10 regional clubs with over 100 local offices. The association covered 22 states and multiple time zones – from the East Coast of the U.S. all the way to the West Coast and as far away as Alaska.

The association had a membership growth/retention problem. I love problems, so this was exactly in my sweet spot. It had experienced a three-year run of declining membership growth. The board was not happy, as you can imagine. So the leadership team members knew they needed to get the teams inside the organization engaged. They knew that many of the answers to turning around the membership decline were inside the organization. They also knew they needed to seek expertise from the outside to get the team engaged with a plan.

Because of my 20 years' working inside associations, I was retained to guide the teams and develop a way to turn around the membership challenge. First, we completed an initial assessment and brainstormed how to turn obstacles into opportunities for membership growth. We established SMEs (subject matter experts) – what I coined "Tiger Teams." The Tiger Teams allowed everyone to contribute his or her ideas and to learn from each other. This platform was a great medium where growth could bring new opportunities. Our joint efforts resulted in significantly improving the member experience, operational improvements, and retention strategies.

The combination of the teams' collective strengths enabled membership growth to exceed an already aggressive goal by nearly 20 percent in that first year!

The Tiger Teams continued to remain engaged and, as their chair, we exceeded goals for the next three consecutive years. The Association won the National award for the highest net membership growth in the federation. The Tiger Teams energized the entire organization, in all 22 states, to believe in the power of engaging others.

The value of engaging others cannot be overstated. Employee engagement is a powerful way to help your organization achieve more and, at the same time, show your leaders, employees, and members/customers, how much you value them.

I don't tell you my story of membership growth to impress you. I told you the story to impress upon you that, as leaders, we have to step up and lead with a culture of success. Through the valuable quality of engagement, the whole association not only achieved the immediate goal for growth but also established a culture for ongoing, future success.

We live in a world where everyone wants to belong. We are social creatures; so not only in business do we seek to belong to a team or to find a way to add value, but in our personal lives as well. Regardless of where we are, leaders must be intentional in their quest to add value by seeking to engage others.

When I was thinking of how best to illustrate the power of engagement, I thought I would ask two of my friends for their thoughts. The first is my friend Crystal Underwood. Why Crystal? Well, I knew that she had spent her whole life adding value to others, specifically children, through her puppet ministry and I wondered how she ever got interested in this area.

It was Christmastime in the Bahamas. Crystal's "Uncle Bill" would dress up as Santa Claus for the children of the community in Nassau. Uncle Bill was not really her uncle; Crystal called him that because he treated her like family. So, this particular year her Uncle Bill asked her to be his little Santa's helper. Crystal thought: "Me, a kid who has a disability? I have cerebral palsy, and he still asked me? I can't believe it!" And she worried: "Could I really be Santa's helper? How would people feel if someone like me was Santa's helper?" Uncle Bill assured Crystal that it would be okay. So she put on her green elf pants and donned her elf green parallel construction hat, and off they went.

They visited children from all walks of life. The first visit was to a crisis center with 50 to 100 children from homes where they had been physically or mentally abused. The children's eyes lit up when Uncle Bill and Crystal handed them their handsomely wrapped presents. They played games and sang songs of the season. Their visit brought smiles to each of the children's faces.

Next, Crystal and Uncle Bill visited children at the Lyford Cay International School. These were children of wealthy parents who did not want for anything. They got equally as excited when Santa and Crystal, his little helper, arrived at the school. They happily accepted their presents. Crystal and Uncle Bill also visited a middle-class area park where the children ran to meet them and feasted on hamburgers and hot dogs while they merrily unwrapped their gifts.

In every one of their visits something amazing happened. The children didn't mind that Crystal was different than they were; in fact, they didn't even notice. Crystal's experience made a great impact on her life. You see, because Uncle Bill encouraged her to participate, because he allowed her to interact with the children, because the children welcomed her and connected with her, Crystal was inspired to become more involved in helping and serving. After that experience, she volunteered to teach at the local church on Sundays. Crystal wanted to give back, and not let her disability keep her from contributing. Not only did she want to contribute but she also wanted to be the one to come alongside the children, and teach them that all children matter, even if they are different. That day Uncle Bill taught Crystal that she did have real value.

Engaging with others can happen in life or business. We can give other people the opportunity to feel real value and to be valued. When we do this, we are what I would say is a Valuable Leader.

My second friend is Roy Hindman, who lives in North Carolina. Roy had a long, successful career in business and, on one of my many trips to visit his family, I had the privilege to listen to Roy as he shared several stories. I enjoy talking with him because he has such a welcoming demeanor. Currently retired, he spends his time photographing the scenic areas of his state and spending time with his family, which includes a lovely wife and two dogs.

Roy retired at age 67 after a sales career that spanned 42 years, working at both levels of selling: first as a salesman and then as a manager and vice president. He found sales to be much like a competitive sport. When people are part of a team, the more the team works together, encourages, and supports each other, the more effective and successful the team will be.

When I asked Roy about sharing the story of a person who he believes has been a Valuable Leader in his life, Roy immediately thought of such a leader: Bob Chaudoin, his manager and the vice president of sales. Roy's story also demonstrates the value of engagement and the benefits that come when leaders get their employees involved.

Roy recalled that one of the best managers he ever worked with was Bob, a person who really understood the necessary traits of a Valuable Leader, and, most importantly, Roy recalled how Bob spent time with every salesperson, getting to know each person as an individual, determining each one's strengths and weaknesses. Bob's interaction with his team was based on what he had learned by spending time with each member.

Roy remembers a specific sales meeting he attended early in his relationship with Bob. His divisional sales team was one of four nationally and at the time was ranked third in sales accomplishments toward their annual goal. Instead of berating his team members for not being where they all wanted to be in the national standings, Bob told the entire team: "My success as a manager is totally based on your individual success. I will do all I can to help each of you achieve your individual sales goals. As each of you succeed, we as a team will succeed and then I will be successful."

This was not a new management approach for Bob; it was how he did his job. Roy recalls: "Bob would always remind us of the importance of our individual sales contribution to the team goal and that we had his support to help us refocus on what we needed to do to achieve our goals." The end result was that the team ended the year as the top-performing team in the national standings!

Roy says, "I don't believe you can be a truly successful leader unless you are willing to be a mentor first. Great leaders are mentors, counselors, coaches, motivators, and role models with a sincere desire to enhance the success of others." And that's exactly what Roy's manager did for his fellow teammates and for himself.

Roy's story emphasizes the need for employee engagement. His story also demonstrates that employee engagement starts at the top. The leader must be engaged with the team and show the way. Bob made each person feel that his or her contribution was pivotal to the success of the team. Employees need to feel they are important to have a genuine desire to become engaged. I guess today I understand why I always felt so welcomed at Roy's home. He is that kind of leader, someone who is sure to include others and make them feel valued. I know, because on each of my visits to his beautiful home in the windy hills of western North Carolina, Roy makes me feel like I am family.

How does one engage with the members of his or her team? I would suggest this: Start with a collaborative effort. Take a few minutes now and write out your thoughts about the following action items. How will you begin to cultivate a culture that engages? You can take these types of actions:

1. Brainstorm ideas with team members and give credit where credit is due. Help others shine!

2. Be inclusive rather than exclusive and acknowledge the contributions of all. Celebrate each win, no matter how small the victory.

3. Set your team goals based on areas where you have the greatest opportunity for all to benefit. Remember success does take a village.

Your next step awaits; see you there.

Power to Engage.

Are you a leader who is engaged? Are your team members engaged?

You can have the most talented organization and be the most well-known leader and it all means nothing if your organization is not engaged. Head here for the information on how to SOAR to create an environment that is not only engaged but also valued.

Visit **TheValuableLeader.com**.

CHAPTER 6. REFLECT: LEARN FROM A TASTE OF THE PAST

"The unexamined life is not worth living."

— Socrates

THE GREATNESS OF VALUABLE LEADERS HAPPENS OVER TIME, WHEN THEY TAKE TIME TO REFLECT AND LEARN FROM THEIR PAST. They reflect on what they did right and what they did wrong. They reflect on what they did well and where they could have done better. They not only contemplate their past, but they also examine how they impacted the lives of others in their past. They ask themselves, "What is the difference that I made to my teams? What is the difference that I made in my family and community?" The definition of reflection in the sense of introspection is "to show, make known, or to think carefully about something."

The sixth step on your path to becoming a Valuable Leader is to hit the "pause" button in your life and REFLECT. Valuable leaders take time to *reflect*.

When we drive our cars, we are told to keep our eyes on the road and observe what lies ahead, which is, after all, the direction we are headed. I completely agree and that's why I value the quality of envisioning the future outlined in Chapter 2. However, while the Valuable Leader spends more time imagining the future, he or she also knows the value of reflection. Valuable leaders don't forget their past while they build their future. In fact, I would propose that valuable leaders build their future with great consideration from lessons learned in their pasts.

You might have heard that "experience is the best teacher." I have come to challenge that statement and have learned that the examined experiences in life are the best teachers.

Leaders who reflect think about the lessons they have learned. My path to becoming a Valuable Leader has taught me to always take time to reflect. I have learned to look in the rear mirror of my life and search for the golden nuggets that I can refine to improve the value of my leadership. There is gold in our experiences, and wise leaders stop to search for the gold and to apply those nuggets they learned from the lessons of life to their future.

To transform yourself and to find your value, you must reflect on your past, serve your present, and envision your future. Looking inward allows you to evaluate your strengths and identify problematic traits that can devalue you as a leader.

When you take the time to examine yourself, take time for self-reflection about your performance, you are admitting that you know you are not perfect as a leader. In fact, if you have any thought than that a leader is first and foremost a learner, then I want to encourage you to ask your staff members how you could add value to them on their jobs.

All leaders, regardless of where they are on their path of leadership, need to be growing. We live in a dynamic society. Leaders cannot lead well if they don't change, and to change you need to grow. Yet growth without intention, without reflection, is like a bird saying, "I cannot fly." The bird can fly. The bird simply needs to learn to flap its wings and jump.

To increase your value, you need to reflect on your value. Self-awareness gives you the ability to understand yourself today – your emotions, strengths, weaknesses, and all the qualities that make you into the person you are – and the person you will be tomorrow. Self-awareness is something you owe to yourself and to those who value you.

As the leader, you must evaluate and reflect on the performance of your staff as well. If you were holding your team to an evaluation of its performance, would you not also do the same for you and your value as a leader? Our society has taught us to evaluate and reflect on tasks and how we are measuring up to the things at work or home. Leaders have an opportunity to evaluate what their own value is to each person on their team. Are you examining how you are adding value to others? Does you team consider you to be a leader who adds value? If tomorrow came without you, would your leadership be missed? Answering these questions can help you reflect on your value as a leader.

With so many books written for leaders, I am sure you must be wondering "why another book?" I thought about that too when I was challenged to write down my seven steps to greater growth, value, and influence. I truly don't believe this is just another leadership book. In fact, I would say this is more about the leader than the position of leadership. This is about the people who added value to others and were then recognized with the distinction of being leaders. This book brought to life the seven steps that help everyone and anyone create value as a leader. All of these seven steps, told in the personal stories shared in this book, I believe encompass the Valuable Leader.

These seven steps build upon the importance of emotional intelligence. There has been more and more research done around emotional intelligence. Taking time to reflect opens your mind to see yourself where you are, and what you can be. Leaders like Aristotle and Socrates tell you and me that self-reflection is too great a value to pass up. To quote Shakespeare "To thine own self be true." Wisdom is when we can truly say we know our value, not simply that we think we are adding value.

The importance of reflection is not a new concept. Confucius, a Chinese teacher, editor, politician, and philosopher, of the spring and autumn period of Chinese history, said:

"By three methods we may learn wisdom: First by reflection, which is the noblest; second by imitation, which is the easiest; and third by experience, which is the bitterest."

When you become a leader who people want to follow, you have learned the value of self-reflection. Great leaders are the ones who know the power of removing their blind spots. They are the ones who look in the mirror and ask, "Would I work for me? Am I the kind of leader others want to follow, or do others have to follow me?"

What would you say to yourself at this very moment? Reflect on yourself as a leader and your role as a leader in your life and business. Are you a Valuable Leader?

When I coach other leaders (seasoned or emerging), I share with them an exercise and strategic framework where they do one-to-one reflection. Reflecting is a great way for them to pause and think back about their impact as a leader. During the development of this book I had the opportunity to work with an emerging leader – a millennial who, at that time in her life, was struggling to find her value. She engaged me as her coach because she was stuck and wanted to break through the barriers to find her true leadership value. We did that. By looking back, through open and honest conversations, assessments, reflection exercises, and probing questions, this emerging leader was able to see the gaps in her leadership ability. She discovered that the seven steps outlined in this book were fundamental to helping her gain greater growth, value, and influence. She is on her way to becoming a Valuable Leader.

Clarity is a powerful tool in helping to move you forward. Perhaps you have been stuck too, or maybe you are there today, mired in trying to find your value and how you can be valued as a leader. Maybe you have been passed over for a promotion or missed out on a new job opportunity. Maybe you can't get your young children to share in your perspective of what's best for the family. Don't lose hope. Be encouraged, my friend. There are seasons for everything and this is but a season for you to gain greater growth, value, and influence. The value you need to lead is inside of you; you simply need to uncover it.

If you are someone who has uncovered your value, bravo! You are one of the few and mighty who know the importance of continuing on your path. Being a Valuable Leader is only the beginning, not an end in itself. A Valuable Leader is someone you become, not something you do. You must be intentional, like the story of my millennial leader. As for me, I have been on the path to becoming a Valuable Leader my whole life. Every day I learn something new about my value and my leadership. Every day, I learn that I can be a better leader today than I was yesterday. The choice is mine. The choice is yours. To be a Valuable Leader means that you are striving to be a better leader every day.

You don't have to travel the path of leadership alone. All great leaders know that they can and do benefit from having a coach or mentor to help them. A coach is the one who will help you reflect on your experiences to build a path forward towards your dreams. Remember the hit song "I Can See Clearly Now" by Johnny Nash? That's one of the many benefits in having an executive coach. You learn to see things from a clearer perspective. You reflect on your experiences and bring to life a new sense of clarity, a better perspective.

Up until now, I never really had a good grasp on what an executive coach was for or even did for that matter. We have all heard of coaches for football, baseball, and other professional sports or even coaches for business professionals climbing the corporate ladder. So, what's the big deal about having an executive coach? Aren't executive coaches exclusively for the executives of a company? How is having an executive coach going to make me see things any clearer? Isn't an executive coach purely a person who tells you what to do?

Let me share a little story from a "growing season" in my corporate career, a time when I needed to reflect on where I was on my path, on where I needed to go, and what I needed to do differently to get there.

In 2013, in an instant, I was downsized! Well, not really me personally, but my position. The company went through a merger and my position was eliminated. Although the elimination of my position was not personal, the impact felt personal to me. This season of my career afforded me the opportunity to take advantage of investing in an executive coach.

Like me, you may have personally faced

the loss of a job or, if not, you know someone who has been impacted this way. As a part of my outplacement package, I was given the chance to work with an executive coach, but I failed to fully understand and take advantage of the valuable services of this expert. I flat out didn't understand how the coach-client relationship worked. My coach would ask me questions without giving me any answers. Sure, he was a nice guy and all and met one-to-one with me each week, but each time all I got was question after question: "What did you do this week to accomplish your goals? How do you think you should do that? Why do you feel stuck?" I felt like all I got were questions, and what I really wanted were answers! You know, like when the coach of the football team says to the player "Go do it this way." Isn't that what my executive coach was supposed to be doing?

I realize I didn't know what a coach really was; back then I had it completely wrong. Because I never understood the process, I became frustrated from all those probing questions, and, instead of listening, well, I downsized my coach and embarked on my journey alone.

Fast forward to 2016. I was on a new discovery of reflecting on my leadership journey and finding my value as a leader. I decided that I needed an outside view to get a clearer perspective on my journey. My coach was a member of my American Marketing Association local chapter, someone who was a very successful trainer and coach in his own right. He explained in plain language, more like a friend than a coach, that there was a real difference between a coach and a mentor: "When a person shares information with you, that person is teaching or training; when a person shares their experience with you, that person is mentoring; but when a person is asking questions and listening deeply to the answers, that's called coaching." On went the light bulb! That's what my executive coach was doing: he was asking me those tough questions, trying to get me thinking. The problem was not with my executive coach; the problem was actually with me. The answers were within – what I needed to do was to stop, and take time to think, and to reflect.

Today I understand more clearly that the coaching process has three objectives. To help you:

Create a greater awareness for yourself.

Increase responsibility for yourself.

Develop accountability for yourself.

Coaching is not about the coach. When you are the coach your focus is on the player or the client. A coach does more listening and less talking, letting the client set the agenda. The coach is fully present but is actively listening deeply, asking questions and building rapport. A coach uses the process to drive meaningful change both for today and tomorrow.

Today, I am a Certified Coach – how ironic. Yet, as a coach myself, I have a coach. A coach who helps me focus on my areas for continued growth; a coach who knows the questions to ask me so I can reflect and learn. The greatest investment you can make is an investment in yourself. What's inside of you? What you learn and develop are the gifts that no one can take away. Nurturing those gifts is the difference between being great and being valuable!

Perhaps you want your leadership to be so valuable that your organization, your teams, and your other leaders realize your value. Perhaps you have realized your own value. You are a Valuable Leader and you know what is involved in giving value to others. Your leadership ability will determine your effectiveness and your impact on your organization. In order to grow your company or your team, you must first grow yourself. You know, you must continue to "lift up your level of influence" so that you can expand your value as a leader.

Great leaders know the value of having an executive coach, a coach who can help you grow, see things with more clarity, and help you answer the questions that can improve your consciousness and help you to move forward. For a clearer perspective, invest in yourself. For things to change for you, they must change *in* you.

Leadership is an individual goal. I am continually amazed that businesses allow time for reflection and review of their plans relative to financial and strategic goals but fall short on reflecting upon their leadership value. They constantly reflect and ask how the company performed relative to its budget and goals. What about the goals for their leaders' development? Perhaps the responsibility of a leader's development falls more on the leaders themselves versus their organizations. After all, leaders must step up to lead first themselves and then give what they have to foster the development of others. We should look at each new season as a time to see how we performed as a leader, and how we can improve. This I believe is a key difference between good leaders and valuable leaders.

Change is the only thing that is changing. Don't be afraid to make changes as you go along, but make those changes based on insight into avenues where you can increase your value. Change for the sake of changing is not productive. We must be intentional, with a sense of purpose.

To become a Valuable Leader, you must

take 100 percent responsibility for your leadership growth. When you are leading with value, you own your results: the good and the bad, the successes and, yes, the failures.

Take a closer look at yourself. This may sound easy, especially when we reflect on the good experiences in our life. A Valuable Leader has learned that the greatest growth comes out of the examination of past mistakes, which is never easy. Trust me on this because I know first hand you will not want to see all of the things revealed by your leadership style. Remember leaders are not born; they are created along the way. We will each make mistakes, but when we take time to reflect on our growth and adjust for improvement, we begin to refine our value. We become like a diamond. We are constantly being cut and polished to become more beautiful and worth more than the original form. Remember, a diamond is made. The stone was not always valuable. The diamond started out as a rough stone, but, through refinement, cutting, and polishing it was formed into a gem:

That's the path of a Valuable Leader.

Leadership is much like the diamond. We all start out a rough self-made manager – responsible for others and their performances, responsible for getting the job done. Then through continuous reflection we uncover our own value. Our refinement from a rough-edged manager to a multi-faceted leader begins to unfold. We start to see the soft skills needed to gain greater impact and influence in the lives of others. We begin to care about others and want the best for them.

Through cutting off the bad habits and refining the value, we can polish the skills needed to lead. We move from a leadership position into a leader of people. Leading starts with the individual, and is unique to each one of us. How we define our path is up to us. But define we must. The honor of being a leader is too great a responsibility to decide that one will stand by the road sign and not travel forward.

When was the last time you reflected and considered your value? Stopped doing, stopped trying, and, stopped all the busy-ness of life? As a leader, you know that there is great value in spending less of your time asking "What am I not doing right?" Instead ask, "What am I doing well? How can I spend my time better? How can I help my team members spend their time better?"

Let me share several experiences from one of the leaders whom I have learned from on my path to becoming a Valuable Leader. His name is Don Gagnon. I met Don several years before, but it was during the period of 2014–2017 that I truly came to value Don as a leader. Don writes of his experiences in working with a seasoned leader early in his career who understood the value of reflection, and later in his career, he shares his reflection of working with an emerging leader who too had the foresight to invest time in reflecting on the experiences of others.

After graduating from college, Don worked at the Associated Grocers of NE (AG), a wholesale food distributor servicing grocery stores of all sizes in New England. Don spent ten years at AG and held several positions with increasing and diverse responsibilities over that time. Throughout his tenure with AG he always reported to the same VP. This VP's name was Mike and he was a "seasoned veteran" of the business.

Mike had spent his entire career in the retail food business and understood all the various needs of retailers better than most people in the industry. He was a very reflective leader. Mike would spend time with Don recounting his experiences and then relate them to the task at hand. Mike impressed him with his willingness to take time to share his learning with him, which helped Don to grow. He taught Don a valuable lesson: always take time to reflect and share. Because of Don's experiences with Mike he learned that leaders must take time to sit down with each staff member who reports directly to them, and share the lessons learned, because those same lessons could be useful to others on their current projects.

After his time at AG, Don then moved on to work at several locations for the American Automobile Association (AAA), where he spent the next 33 years. This time, he worked for a "new and emerging" general manager, Walter. Walter was from the corporate office and had not previously spent any time in the field. Walter took the approach that they would learn together, and learn they did! Essentially, each day they reflected on the past and questioned every aspect of the business. Each of them wanted to learn how things operated and why they functioned as they did. Don recalls, "It turned out to be a great way to learn about the needs of the business from a great group of dedicated managers."

Don came away from that experience appreciating the value of institutional knowledge in helping to evaluate current opportunities. He shares: "While one must respond to changes in the marketplace, it is important to understand what has made you successful to this point in time. It is important to always take time to reflect."

Don's story is a great example that illustrates the value of reflection. Regardless of where we are in our career, we can always apply the learning from our experiences and the experiences of others. As I reflect on my three years working with him, I fondly remember many candid conversations with Don at board and team meetings. I remember Don as a leader who gave so much value that you would be hard-pressed to find anyone who knew him saying they would not work with him. He was that kind of leader; one who I believe everyone would want to follow. I am proud to say he is one of my Valuable Leaders.

There are many leaders adding value to others; I believe we only need to take time to find them. I found such a leader during my journey as a professional speaker with the National Speakers Association. This leader is my newfound friend, John Rollins. When I asked John to contribute a story to the book, I am pretty sure I saw tears in his eyes. I was humbled because I knew he had so much value to offer.

This is a story where my friend reflects on the value of leadership with a heart full of gratitude. Don't misunderstand me; John has had a very challenging life, with tough times and times he just felt that life was not fair, but, all the while John has maintained a positive attitude, adding value to each person he encounters. I would like to include John's story here:

John would say, "If I had a nickel for every time I heard someone say that, 'Life is not fair,' I would be financially set. That statement is so true. There really is nothing fair about life." John was convinced that was the way life should be as he thought more about that statement.

During his parents' retirement ceremony, people shared stories about how poor his family was during his childhood. John says, "But I would not trade a day of my life with anyone that I know." Today he understands that every moment, every shared meal, every pair of second-hand clothes, every low-cost or free lunch – the entire experience for him – was priceless.

His life has not been fair, although he feels blessed beyond anything he could ever imagine. He has two loving parents, a loving and supportive wife, adorable children, and a delightful grandson. He and his siblings enjoy each other's company and always go the extra mile to help out whenever there is a need. The family support structure his parents provided was unlike any he had ever seen. John enjoys great health and feels truly valued. He has been truly favored throughout his life. For John those surroundings created a rare and valued environment.

Calvin Dean was his older brother. Priscilla Anne was his older sister. These two of siblings both died at an early age: Calvin died before John was born and his earliest memory in life was Anne's funeral. He never knew his father's parents. His best friend in high school committed suicide while in college. He lost friends, relatives, and mentors. In fact, his whole family has had its share of tragedy. Out of these situations, the relationships they had with each other grew closer and became their greatest treasure. This made John come to realize that "family matters."

Many people use the reasoning that they are a product of their environment. John believes that there are cases where there may be some truth to those sentiments. But he also understands that each of us has been afforded an opportunity that is unavailable to any of the rest of God's creation: We can choose our response to our situations. Leaders do just that!

Although John believes fully in the "creation" version of man's existence as opposed to a "big bang" theory of evolution, he does agree that there is logic to the "survival of the fittest" concept. There are universal laws that apply and there are consequences for complying with and for violating these laws. One of the laws that he believes creates an attitude of appreciation is an understanding that adversity is the polishing cloth that creates character. To borrow a tired cliché: "Hard times can make you bitter or hard times can make you better." John feels each individual owns the choice. A person might ask, "What about those people who are victims through no fault of their own?" John's response is this, "In one way or another, we all have been put in situations or we will be put in situations where we could become a victim. That is the way it is. Life is not fair."

There are situations where John's heart is moved with compassion for people who are involved in calamities over which they have little or no control. There are other people who create unfortunate situations through their own actions. We are all one wrong decision away from having our lives turned upside down. John often repeats: "The only difference between my life and the lives of everyone else is the decisions – those that have been made by me, those that have been made about me, and those that have been made for me. That's the beauty of life – God has given everyone a chance to choose."

John offers this thought as he reflects on all his experiences: "I realize that life is priceless. MasterCard had the right idea when it said there are some things that money can't buy, but other things are 'priceless.'"

What a powerful story that shows the efficacy of reflection. Sometimes when you look back and examine your life, the lessons you have learned, the choices you have made, you find experiences you wish you could go back and change. Or maybe, like John, you believe it is because of the twists and turns that you encounter, you are the person or leader you have become today and conclude: "I wouldn't change one thing." Regardless, I believe that John is showing us that when we reflect, we take the time to see the good, the bad, and yes, even the ugly. We must take time to see value in everything. The choice is yours; the choice is mine. Leaders know that they must choose!

I have come to appreciate that there is worth in everything, but searching out the value does take time. That's why I value the art of reflection. One of the leaders I admire most is Jim Rohn. Jim says,

"Time is more valuable than money. You can get more money, but you cannot get more time."

Tragically, most people focus on the value of money over the value of time. Perhaps you can relate. What if, for one moment, you reflect with me on the value of time compared to the value of money?

Everyone, regardless of our leadership level, gets 24 hours in a day. Let's say you work eight hours. I know what you are thinking, "No one works eight hours a day," but let's say you work eight hours. Let's say that you sleep eight hours a night in one day. Again, I know what you are thinking, "Nobody gets eight hours of sleep anymore in a day," but, work with me. That leaves eight more hours remaining in a 24-hour day. How are you investing your time? Do you take time to reflect on where your time is being invested?

Are you achieving your goals: at work, at home? Are you accomplishing the things that are important to you? Are you investing the time you have with the people who matter the most to you? When we take time to reflect, we take the time to see where we are making a positive difference, where we are missing out, and where we need to change.

Time is precious, and leaders need to reflect on the time we have. We also need to efficiently and effectively use the time we have with our families, and the time we have with our teams. Peter Drucker, educator, management consultant, and author, whose writings contributed both to the philosophical and practical foundations of modern business, penned the following:

"Nothing else distinguishes effective executives [leaders] as much as their tender loving care of time."

Have you assessed the value of your time?

We live in an age of technology, where there are so many gadgets designed to save us time. Yet we are always saying, "I need to manage my time better," or "I need to spend time with my children this weekend," or "I will kill time until my doctor's appointment."

Friends, don't "manage" time, don't "spend" time, and don't "kill" time. *Invest time.*

Valuable leaders learn to value time.

When was the last time you took time to reflect on your value, your self-worth and that of others in your life? Perhaps now would be a good time to start. Right this moment! Take out your piece of paper and grab a pen or turn to the Notes page in this book. Ask yourself these three questions:

1. What did I do today that made a positive impact on someone?

2. Who did I remember to thank for a small act of kindness?

3. What would I like to achieve tomorrow that I did not achieve today?

Keep thinking, keep reflecting: there is so much to see on your path to becoming a Valuable Leader.

Lead on with the next step.

Check Your Rear View Mirror.

Do you see things clearly? Do you examine your past to help you for the future?

You can't change your past, but by working together, I will give you the tools to take you on a path forward to where you want to be. Find out how.

Learn more about how coaching can add value in my exclusive video series.
Go to **TheValuableLeader.com**.

CHAPTER 7. SERVE: HAVE A HEART FOR LEADERSHIP, PUT OTHERS FIRST

"To handle yourself, use your head; to handle others, use your heart."

— Eleanor Roosevelt

A VALUABLE LEADER HAS A SERVANT'S HEART AND PUTS OTHERS FIRST. To serve means, "to provide help, to assist others." Yes, people who provide service are generally called servants. Servitude is, my friends, a noble pursuit and calling. When you value service, you are a leader who knows the 18-inch rule. That rule states that the distance from your head to your heart is only approximately 18 inches.

The seventh step on your path to

becoming a Valuable Leader is to SERVE. Valuable leaders *serve*.

How ironic that, for as long as anyone can remember, leaders have always been the ones with position, title, and people to "serve" them. Over time, research has found that real leaders are the ones who serve others – not the ones being served.

Real leaders value the impact they make on the lives of others. We are all leaders when we serve. Maybe this upside-down philosophy of leadership is hard to grasp. However, when you lead with a determination to help other people – your family, friends, employees and your community at large – you are currently considered "a servant leader."

Servant leaders become valuable leaders when they exhibit all of the seven values or characteristics outlined in this book. Yes, everyone can become a Valuable Leader. The value of service is the point at which the leader puts aside his or her individual self-serving needs in favor of the needs of others. A leader's focus is on meeting the needs of others by serving them. There is a famous line in a Star Trek movie that goes, "The needs of the many outweigh the needs of the few."

Let me share a story that is very personal in nature and includes my recollections and those of many people whose lives were touched by one man. If you asked most people, they would say this man was the most humble example of a servant leader they would ever personally know. The man I refer to was Wilfred Sawyer, my stepfather.

Many people saw Wilfred as a man who embodied the concept of service. He came from very modest beginnings and had one older brother and a sister. Wilfred was the baby of his family. He was not a tall man in stature. He spoke with a lisp and walked with a slight limp, yet he was known and loved by so many because Wilfred was truly a servant leader. He lived his life with a 100 percent focus on other people. Everyone was important to Wilfred. He never used people or stepped over people to get ahead. He never sought to get glory for himself.

He worked hard all of his life but his toiling wasn't solely about the money, because he didn't really get paid a large salary. He wasn't trying to be the most famous or even the most well known person in his hometown, but you would be hard-pressed to find someone who didn't know him. He never had any people reporting directly to him, yet he influenced many people with his attitude of service. In fact, Wilfred was somewhat of a leadership giant, because every day he worked hard serving everyone he encountered. He would clean toilets, be a bus driver, sweep the floor or greet people, always with a smile on his face and a song in his heart. He made you feel special and was truly happy to be of service.

For those who would never have the opportunity to meet him, people might say "It's more your loss than his." He was a man of true godly character. Wilfred was a Valuable Leader.

What can I say about such a Valuable Leader who could help you and me strive to live a life that has tremendous influence today and makes an eternal impact tomorrow? Perhaps all that I can say is we should wake up every day, put a smile on our faces, keep a song in our hearts, and serve people. Be a Valuable Leader by serving others, like Wilfred did.

How do you serve as a leader? Well, with all the leadership books published there is much that is open to interpretation on this subject. Somehow experienced leaders and others who don't believe they are leaders, but want to be, are still searching for the secret.

Breaking news! Leadership has gotten a bad rap mostly because it continues to be tagged with the title or position of the person – not the value of the person. I believe that *The Valuable Leader* is the one who serves with a real sincerity. Valuable leaders are not doing so as a means to achieve their own personal power or purely for their own personal gain. That's simply plain old manipulation and should be redacted from every leadership book and never be a part of any leader's legacy.

A servant leader thinks more of others and believes in their abilities. Servant leaders invest in the gifts they see in people and work to grow and develop their talents. People will do more for you when you show you care about them and you want to help them. Helping others is a mindset of the teacher as well as the student. When you serve, you are a leader who is walking shoulder to shoulder with your team. You don't believe that you are above your team or at the top looking down on them. You act as the team builder, and once the team members are ready to play ball, you get out of the way if needed or you pitch in and help right on par with them. You step back out of the spotlight and onto the sidelines and let the team shine.

Serving others and stepping aside to allow others to lead is not new, because I believe the most Valuable Leader of the Christian faith was, and is Jesus Christ. He is the best example of a servant leader in history. Christ did not see himself alone at the top, nor was he afraid to be of service to others even to the point of washing their feet. He used towels – not titles – to build the members of his team. He served them and prepared them each day to lead, and, in so doing, his team ultimately went on to impact millions of others for the greater good.

But how do we acquire this value of service? First, service starts with the understanding that no one member of the team is of more value or of more importance than another. People who embrace this view live the proverb "The first will be last and the last will be first." With the mindset that to be first, or to translate "to be the leader," you must first be the servant or "follower." You must have a strong desire to serve and seek out ways to live out that desire. You must learn to give away, and not expect or assume a return. Once you make the decision that you want to serve, it is then that you actively make the choice to do exactly that, to serve. Your focus is on the success of others and how you can help them succeed. The milestones achieved by others on your team are the best measures of success for any leader. *The Valuable Leader* is a successful leader because he or she has learned the value of service to others and elevating their performance.

You don't need to try and serve everyone to change the world. You simply need to start right where you are. Start serving those you meet and work with every day. Service leads from the heart! As a leader your value shines through when you serve. By serving others, you find your true value. You don't "do" leadership. You "live" leadership."

To serve should come naturally to all of

us because we all know the value when we are served. But many organizations are struggling to provide excellent customer and member service. Why? I believe there exists a gap in the culture of the organization, and the gap is the servant-leader mindset.

Many people belong to groups, clubs, and associations because they see the value from that business model. Service by the group is expected; it's not just an add-on. Rather, service is an added value. We have all heard the slogans "It pays to be a member," or "Membership has its privileges." This is talking about value, right? The value proposition of your business is the promise that you will deliver on what you say you will deliver. But service is beyond mere words; it's about what we do for others that truly is at the heart of the matter. Having a servant's mentality is about living a life filled with humility. When employees adopt an attitude of service within their organizations, it signals to the leaders that they have filled the gap in the company's culture. They have employees who are engaged and want to be a part of the solution, not the problem. They have employees who feel that their leaders value them and want to serve.

Everyone is in the service business, no matter what our chosen path may be! As valuable leaders, our attitude should be no different than that of a servant: to seek ways in which we can help others in their daily lives.

Keep in mind that no matter the situation, we each have a duty to serve. We must serve our teams, our boards, our volunteers, and our members or customers. We must serve our families, our friends, and our communities. As a leader, first and foremost, we must serve!

When I reflect on my growth as a leader, I remember a time when I came face-to-face with the concept of service, the value of being a servant leader. Here is my story:

Early in my corporate career, I had no idea of the concept of being a leader, let alone that a leader was one who was a servant. I thought that leadership simply consisted of the everyday actions taken by my leader. Not actions taken by me. Actions like making decisions or providing vision for our company. That was my leader's responsibility. I thought that a leader gave the directions and everyone in the organization followed him or her. Perhaps you have thought that same way about the leaders you know. But these daily actions are only a part of the many responsibilities of a leader.

As a young professional, I was given a leadership role early in my career. Over time my worldview of what leadership is has changed. I once thought leadership was all about the leader. I quickly learned that being a leader is so much more than championing a cause. I had valuable experiences with a few great leaders and then there were those experiences with leaders who were not so good. I actually found more opportunities to learn from poor leaders than the great ones. And learn I did! Those poor leaders often had more of an influence on me than I expected. The smart leader knows better than to repeat the lessons of a poor leader.

Like learning from my own failures – "missteps," as I prefer to call them – I learned from those who may not have been the best examples of what a leader should be. Don't get me wrong; I always aspired to be like the great leaders I had known. They inspired me to grow, to become a better leader – even a great one. But those lessons learned from the poor choices of other leaders, and, sadly the poor choices I made myself, made me even more determined to avoid that style of leadership and the pitfalls that came along with it going forward. A burning desire was created in me to discover and better understand why there were leaders who were great, and then other leaders who were not.

As much as I hate to admit I made mistakes in my leadership roles, I did. Even with poor leaders showing me what not to do as a leader, I regret to say that I did not always master the leadership role the first time. I made quite a few leadership mistakes in my career. However, my quest to become a better leader propelled me to begin studying the art of leadership, specifically, the types of people we call great leaders. I studied the leadership giants of different eras – even those leaders dating back to biblical times. I sought out mentors who helped me uncover my own personal leadership gifts. I am cognizant of the fact that being a leader can be both simple and complex, and it's bigger than the leader.

If you ask 100 different people what leadership is, you will get over 100 different answers, because the concept of leadership is forever changing. Leadership is not only about business: leadership is about life. A good leader inspires others to live more, love more, and be more. A leader creates a sense of trust because, through service, the leader seeks to understand others first. Leaders seek to do more for others and it is because of actions like these that they themselves are trusted. Leaders modeling the quality of service have become the Valuable Leader.

I would like to share two stories with you to illustrate the concept of how a leader serves, or, better still, what a servant leader is. Deborah Frock, affectionately known as Debi to those who know her well, is a valued friend of mine and I share her story first. Debi's story is one that is more personal in nature.

At the age of six, Debi met the most influential leader in her life, Ella Mae Hart. Miss Ellie was five feet, two inches tall, with short brown hair – a petite woman. She had a soothing, mezzo-soprano voice and was still single at the age of 26. This was her first year as a Sunday school teacher.

Miss Ellie's class consisted of six very different little girls. All of them came from blue-collar families living barely above the poverty level. Miss Ellie would be their teacher for five years, and every month she would arrange a fun outing for them after church, like a trip to the zoo, or maybe a picnic at her house. Being girls on the cusp of hormonal changes, they did not always see eye to eye during these adventures. When squabbles broke out, Miss Ellie used her soothing voice to calm them down and relate a parable from the Bible to teach them a lesson. No matter the outing, Miss Ellie always found a way to make their time together a fun learning experience.

From the beginning it was evident that Miss Ellie loved Jesus and she definitely loved her six girls unconditionally. She always had a smile and a hug for each of them. This unconditional love was a welcome change from Debi's home life. Miss Ellie's example taught the girls to love and respect others and themselves.

Sundays were Debi's favorite day of the week.

Each week Miss Ellie gave the girls an assignment. Sometimes she would ask them to memorize a song or a scripture verse. Songs were easy for Debi, but memorizing verses created a challenge. Miss Ellie encouraged her with small rewards for trying. Soon Debi was able to memorize the verses as easily as a song.

Debi's family moved away during her fourth year with Miss Ellie. True to her nature as a leader Miss Ellie gave Debi a new testament with her favorite verse underlined, and Debi had to read eight chapters before she found the verse, 2 Corinthians 5:17, and this verse has remained a favorite of Debi's. Miss Ellie also continued to invite Debi to be a part of her life. She attended Debi's wedding and Debi attended hers. Miss Ellie never had children of her own but was a leader to many children.

Miss Ellie was a role model who inspired Debi to become a Sunday school teacher, a church soloist, and eventually a missionary to children in Ghana, West Africa. When Debi returned from Ghana in 2007 and shared photos of the children with Miss

Ellie, Miss Ellie pointed to one child and asked, "How can I help make this little girl's life better?" Because of that simple question, Debi's nonprofit, Ghanaian Mothers' Hope, started the child sponsorship program and little Nora was able to attend preschool and kindergarten. All thanks to Miss Ellie.

Debi describes how she has learned to live life fully, love unconditionally, and be all that she was called to be. All because of Miss Ellie's kindness and service as a Valuable Leader.

When I think of another person who is a leader who knows what serving others is about, I remember my lifelong friend, Donna. Having a lifelong friend is not the norm anymore, and I consider myself a very blessed individual to be able to say that Donna continues to be my lifelong friend. Donna and I grew up in Nassau together; we were the best of friends. When she moved with her family to one of the other islands in the Bahamas, a large piece of my heart went with her.

I remember the day she told me she was leaving. We were only about 10 years old – we were kids – and yet my heart still aches when I reflect on that moment. We were two little girls, with two different lives and two different stories. As I started to write this book, she was one of the individuals I wanted to speak to about the characteristics of what I believe make someone a Valuable Leader.

Where did Donna learn the value of service? I wondered this for a long time and, well, I thought I knew the answer: her father. She surprised me with a story about her mother. I was excited to hear more about her mother, all the while, in the back of my mind, thinking that, as a mom herself, Donna is a leader. Let's begin the story with one mother, Anne Mae, who passed the value of service down to her daughter, Donna.

Donna's mother, Annie Mae Roberts Albury-Kittoe, was a leader who knew the value of service, of doing for others despite her own circumstances. At the age of 18, Annie Mae married and was, over time, blessed with ten children. Donna was the baby of the family. There were numerous moves from the family's small island home of Great Guana Cay to the capital city of Nassau and back again.

Often Donna's father would be away from the home, sometimes for weeks at a time, as he worked on a mail boat travelling between islands. Anne Mae had to make sure the house was maintained, the children were all dressed, meals were prepared, and everything ran smoothly. She had to serve in many roles.

There was never a time when Donna's mother did not find herself having to be both a servant and a leader. Then as both her parents aged, Anne Mae needed to serve in another role, as a caretaker for her own mother and father, all while still having children of her own to care for. She willingly took her parents in and cared for them with love.

Annie Mae happily continued her role as a servant when the family moved to Man-O-War Cay, another small island in Abaco. There she supported the family as a seamstress in her sister's island store. Every day, Donna learned the value of service because her mother was a real life example for all her children. The appreciation of serving others turned out to be a lesson that served them well.

Anne Mae would ultimately age and her health declined. The time had come for her children to serve and apply the lessons learned from their mother. They had seen their mother, Annie Mae, move the family from place to place, care for her children, and become a parent to her own mother and father. Seeing this lesson made Donna and her sisters determined to do the same for their mother. Each daughter would take turns serving Annie Mae: cooking, cleaning, and meeting her needs for many years. Donna and her sisters stepped up in the same way their own mom had. Donna often recalls her mother saying: "What is worth doing, is worth doing well." Both Donna and Annie Mae certainly lived out that saying by serving their mothers well.

As her life-long and childhood best friend, I had witnessed for myself how my dear friend always put others before herself. I witnessed how Donna looked after her husband, raised her only daughter, Beth, and was a caretaker for her own mother as well. I felt the need to dig a little deeper into how my dear friend was living out her life as a Valuable Leader.

I wondered what Donna's own daughter, Beth, would say about her mom? Of course, Beth instantly agreed with me – her mom is a Valuable Leader. Beth could not wait to unveil stories of how her mom was a Valuable Leader who lives a life of service.

Beth opens her story by saying: "My mother Donna is a strong leader, with a servant's heart. She is a woman who deeply cares about the wellbeing of others. She often goes out of her way, even becoming uncomfortable, for the sake of putting others first and at ease."

Beth brings to mind so many times when they were invited into other peoples' homes, her mom would be found serving in the kitchen, washing dishes and cleaning up, because Donna thought about how tired her host would feel after cooking and preparing the meal.

Many times Donna could be found sitting with mothers of others because she could both empathize with a caregiver and sympathize with an elderly shut-in. Beth recalls the words of Helen Keller: "So long as you can sweeten another's pain, life is not in vain." And Beth adds, "My mom shows leadership qualities by serving and always putting others first."

Beth says that Donna feels like her accomplishments are so simple. Her mom feels that the things she does are part of a necessary, daily routine. For example, growing up, Donna would often tell Beth of the importance of "leaving things better than you found them."

She taught Beth that, after washing her hands, it only takes a few more seconds to dry up any water around the sink before hanging up the towel. Whether the vanity was dry and the towel picked up beforehand was irrelevant. Beth learned from her mom that taking the time to be thoughtful and serve others takes only a few extra moments on our part, but can make a world of difference to another individual. Beth fondly remembers her mom sitting at the table, writing cards and "thank you" letters. Donna taught Beth that: "People are not interested in prose, but they do crave to know that someone, anyone, cares." Donna taught Beth to lead by doing more than simply the basics. She taught her to "first serve others!"

Beth feels her mom excels as a leader because she is willing to get her hands dirty. She is always busy serving and helping whomever and whenever she could. She sees her mom as a "special woman who put others first by doing more than the basics." Beth watched her mother and learned by example. Beth recalls: "She brought me up to her level and expected me to do the same." To serve just as she did. When Beth thinks of her mom doing her random acts of kindness, giving little bursts of extra effort, she likes to imagine that her mom is "leaving flowers in her wake – tiny blooms of hope where there was once a touch of darkness."

Both Donna and Beth's stories are so intertwined that their stories give us representation of leading by example, how you truly serve and how, in doing so, you teach others to do the same. Service becomes a legacy.

Sometimes we never know the impact we will have on the lives of others: an impact that can be passed down from person to person, even from generation to generation. Perhaps Annie Mae knew how her life impacted her family. Perhaps she did not. One thing is certain, Beth knows the impact her mom had on their family, a legacy that was passed down by her grandmother to her mom, and one that she is passing on to her own daughter, Mollie Iris.

My lifelong friend Donna Marie Albury is a woman of value. A Valuable Leader who has always lived her life serving her family and taking care of them. She has passed down that same spirit that came from her mother to her own daughter, Beth. Donna would never say she is a leader, that's how humble a leader she is. Yet, when you are a Valuable Leader, like Donna, leading others through service is not something you have to work at, serving is a characteristic that comes naturally.

As leaders, we too, are often unaware of what our legacy will be, especially when we take the approach to lead with a service mindset.

When we learn to value ourselves, we can learn to value others. And when we learn to value others, we lead without position, without title, without offices, without power, and without any external force. We lead with value. We lead with something we have deep inside of us that no one can take away. We lead because we are valuable.

When you leave this world, what will others say about your impact, about your life, and most of all, about your value? Today is the day for you to step up and take hold of the value that you have inside, to rediscover the leadership qualities that you want to live out and emulate as you continue your journey to becoming a Valuable Leader.

So what specific actions do you need to take in order to apply the value to serve in leading others?

1. Start with being vulnerable. Reach out to others as individuals and seek to get to know them. Being vulnerable is a risky business, but valuable leaders are brave enough to take the risk.

2. Ask questions about the dreams and desires of others. Think about ways you

can help them achieve their dreams. Invest your time in the development of what's important to someone else.

3. Lend a helping hand early on in your relationship with others. Meet their needs without any expectations of a return. Have a service mindset. Focus on what is important to others, not only on what is important to you. Reach out a hand and assist them because it matters to them. Serve because you value them.

Living your value is your choice.

Serve to Lead.

You can have the most important title and position and it means nothing if people aren't willing to follow you.

Don't miss out! Get more information on how you can learn to lead effectively with a servant's heart.

Visit **TheValuableLeader.com**.

CHAPTER 8. SUMMARY: NOW IT'S YOUR TURN, LEAD ON.

"You never know when a moment and a few sincere words can have an impact on a life."

— Zig Ziglar

Many people claim to be leaders, but only a few truly know the value of their impact. To be a leader is not something you do, but someone you become. Leadership is not something you have, but something you give. You can't turn on and then turn off leadership when you feel the need to do so. To be a leader is an honor and not something any one of us should ever take lightly.

Leadership has existed in civilization for over 6,000 years. Today, more and more books are written on the subject because there is so much more to learn. The role of a leader is never-ending and forever changing. To lead is to make a lasting impact, to change the course of direction for people and give them hope, give them courage, and most of all, give them value. I believe that when we lead with value, we give the greatest gift: an investment in the lives of others and ourselves that is truly invaluable.

As I thought about leaders who have made a lasting impact, I recall my sister, Lilly, telling a story about the impact our grandmother had on her life. How she saw all seven of the qualities of a Valuable Leader in the matriarch of our family.

Lois Merlee Malone, or "Ma" as she was known, was born in the Bahamas on the island of Great Guana Cay in the Abacos to Samuel and Delancy Roberts. She was a woman of humble origins and an only child. When Merlee was a child, her mother died, and she and her father were left to build a life together. Ma learned from her early childhood that she needed to *serve* others. She was dedicated to taking care of her father and then, later in life, she did the same serving her entire family: her husband, children, grandchildren, and so many others. Life on the small island was simple but difficult, and many families made a living by fishing, farming, and carpentry.

Ma was no stranger to tough times. She married while in her teens and was forced to move away from her simple life on the Cay to the "big city" of Nassau. Work was tough to come by because her husband was not a fisherman, so to earn a living and support the family they relocated to Nassau. By the age of 18 her beautiful brown head of hair had turned to a stunning snowy white color, but her beauty remained. Her beauty came from the inside out.

Life in Nassau was not always smooth either. Our grandfather was not able to find steady work as a carpenter and he sought solace in a bottle. Ma was a woman of *action*; she assumed the role as leader of the family and took a job as a sales clerk at a local department store. Working outside the home was the only way to make sure her six children had food to eat and that the bills were paid. Even through all the struggles, Ma never faltered; she pressed on, and kept a smile on her face.

As her children married and had children of their own, our grandmother was determined to *engage* with each one of us through her weekly visit, from house to house. Even though she never learned to drive, she found a ride to our homes because spending time with her children and grandchildren was an important value to her. Our family was close-knit, all because she took the lead and kept each member of the family together, engaged, and informed. She was the living and breathing equivalent of Facebook at the time.

Lilly gives an example of the Sunday afternoons that she would spend with our grandmother. She never knew at the time that those afternoons spent with our grandmother would impact her life for many years to come.

After Sunday church concluded, Ma would get a ride to come and pick up Lilly to take her over to her house. Ma would *listen* as Lilly told her all about what happened during the week and would give her sound advice. They would sing together, play records, or talk about which family birthdays were coming up. They would spend hours together. This quality time with our grandmother was important to Lilly because, of course, like many young teenage girls, she could never agree with our mother. Our grandmother was the one with the listening ear, the one who Lilly knew she could always depend upon.

The hardships in our grandmother's childhood and young adult life would often bubble up in her mind and give her pause. She would *reflect* on those memories and she become more determined to change the family history. She sacrificed daily and quite willingly so her family could have a better life.

Lilly would watch our grandmother do the mending and sew patches on clothes and yearned to learn more about the craft of sewing. Ma would share with Lilly how she wanted Lilly to grow and use her talents. Ma's desire for Lilly to grow and *develop* her talent, coupled with Lilly's yearning, inspired Lilly to enroll in a sewing class in her senior year of high school. Of course, Ma was there to encourage her. Lilly fondly remembers Ma saying: "Children need to learn how to sew." Even though my sister began working as a bookkeeper right out of school, deep inside she heard the voice of Ma encouraging her to develop her talent.

Ma would *envision* how Lilly could earn a living from developing her natural talent to sew. She saw the gifts my sister had at a young age and would consistently encourage her. Today, Lilly credits her love of sewing to our grandmother. My sister has her own successful sewing and upholstery business on a small island in the Abacos.

By now you know that leading is not one specific event; rather, leading is a sequence of events, over a period of time. Yes, moments provide a flicker of insight into the kind of leader you are, but it's important to remember that the combination of all those moments in time develop your character and reveal you as a Valuable Leader.

There is one thread, one important attitude, which should be evident in each of these seven components of a Valuable Leader. What is that thread? I uncovered it as I reflected on my grandmother's life. No matter where she was in her life, she was always a leader who encouraged others. We must always be an encourager.

It became so evident to me during the development of this book. I have met valuable leaders, learned important lessons, and heard incredible stories about people who have impacted the lives of others. They are people who in their own right are valuable leaders. People who knew the value of their leadership and its impact on those they led and others, well, they will never know.

Whose lives are you impacting? And

how?

I would like to share with you one more story: the final story on our path to becoming a Valuable Leader. This story is from Barry Banther. He is the author of more than 50 leadership-training programs. Barry has earned the highest accreditation from the Institute of Management Consultants as a Certified Management Consultant and from the National Speakers Association as a Certified Speaking Professional. Most of all, Barry is a leader who cares. I met Barry at a National Speakers Association event. I knew of him, but, at this specific event, I got to *know* him. Barry was the guest speaker for a workshop I was attending and, while we did not have a lot of time together, the time we did spend together influenced me deeply.

During one of the breaks during the workshop, I approached Barry and asked if he would share a story for my book. He never hesitated. With a humble smile on his face, Barry said, "Yes." And then, he did something I did not expect. He stopped in a room full of people, placed his hand on my shoulder, and asked if he could say a short prayer with me. As a woman of faith, this was a special moment. As Barry prayed, my heart filled with joy and gratitude. What an encouragement that was for me. He prayed for my book, *The Valuable Leader*, and for all of you who have decided to take the steps on the journey to be the Valuable Leader.

That day Barry gave me a gift of encouragement. I want to share that gift with you and hope his story will encourage you, too:

> The most influential people in Barry's life have been those who chose to encourage him. That doesn't mean they ignored his mistakes or let him out of obligations. It means they saw all of him and made the decision to bring out the best in him. Nothing inspires men and women to perform better as a team than the encouraging words of those who lead them.

> Barry believes that through your encouraging words that you bring hope. "It's not the load that breaks you down, it's the way you carry it!" That's how Lou Holtz, one of the top three winningest college football coaches of all time, describes a difficult path. A coach's job is to show the team how to carry the load together. A coach's encouragement will give hope, and that will lighten that load.

> "Hope springs!" You may have heard that phrase before, and it is a notion that has stood the test of time. Solomon, the wise author of the book of Proverbs, wrote these words: "Like apples of gold in settings of silver is a word spoken in right circumstances." Solomon

hinted that well thought-out words spoken in the right tone, and in the right moment, were the key to hope. But where does hope really come from? After decades of observing, evaluating, and coaching leaders, Barry is convinced that hope in the workplace springs directly from the leader. And if it doesn't, then rarely will team members achieve their greatest potential.

Barry shares, "Encouragement breeds confidence, and confidence is the root of all proactive customer-centered leadership." Encouragement may be a simple phrase, a smile, or a pat on the back. But a word of encouragement from you could be the fuel that lights a dream or powers an idea. That's why it's a gift...because so few people are willing to find it, wrap it up, and give it away. Like the valuable leader's other gifts, encouragement has to be given freely without prejudice.

Behind every face we see in leadership is a person who has a fair share of challenges in his or her life, as well as strengths that few people may see. As leaders, we can choose to add to every persons' challenges or help them find hope through their abilities – the choice is yours.

Be encouraged, my friend. There are many people waiting just for you. You and I still have the opportunity to see the value we bring as leaders. We still have the opportunity to bring value into the lives of the people we work with, the people we manage, the people in our families, and the people in our communities. More than ever, we are prepared to step up with greater growth, value, and influence, because we know what a Valuable Leader is.

Today you can be the leader everyone wants to follow. You now know that a little bit of value will go a long way in helping you to be the best leader you can be. You have learned the seven proven steps to bring value into your leadership. To take your leadership beyond the day-to-day routine of business and transform your life into one of impact, regardless of where you lead.

You now know that, as a Valuable Leader, you need to have an ear to hear the sound of leadership, to value what others are saying and to seek first to listen. You need to listen with an ear to understand.

You now know you need to have an eye to see the possibilities. To envision the future, a future that is full with opportunities, not obstacles. You need to give hope to others that all things are possible, if only we believe.

You now know, that for anything to

happen, change must begin with you. You must take action, and sometimes, the decision to act will be based on your gut instinct because that will be all you have. But you know, as the leader, you must be the one who leads others to take action as well.

You now know, that to develop others and yourself is mission critical. Growth is not an option, for you or anyone else. As the leader you must lead the charge for continued growth. You must be intentional about growing.

You now know, you must take the initiative to engage others and lead with compassion. People want to be included and you must be the one to include them. Everyone has value to add and you must help them see, share, and build their value.

You now know, you need to take time to reflect. To look back and examine what lessons you have learned. You must reflect on where you have come from and where you are going. Only then can experience propel you forward.

You now know, you must also serve if you are to lead. You must serve with a heart for people. Others must come first. Leading is not just a choice, it is a privilege. Leading is what leaders do!

Leading others is not for the faint of heart. Leadership is not a "one and done" exercise. Your ability to lead requires an ongoing dedication and a deliberate focus on others. True leaders find their value in seeking out the value of those they lead. That person is the Valuable Leader.

Be the Valuable Leader. Follow all these steps as you lead others, and lead them in a way that encourages them, so that one day they say: "I want to be a Valuable Leader... like you."

LEAD ON!

Show Your Value. Lead On!

Now that you've read the book, it's time to make your next move.

Nothing changes unless we implement the things we've learned. Your journey has just begun. As a Valuable Leader you know that all great leaders continue to grow. Map your path to greater growth, value, and influence.

Get started at **TheValuableLeader.com**.

ABOUT THE AUTHOR

Velma Knowles

Velma Knowles is the Founder and CEO of Leaders Pathway, and is a certified marketer, speaker, trainer, and coach. Born and raised on the island of New Providence in the city of Nassau in the Bahamas, Velma was the baby of her family. She endured hardships in the loss of both her brother and father by the age of eight. Velma used these tough times to develop her sheer sense of determination: determination that drove her to develop a personalized fundraising campaign to raise over $100,000 for college abroad.

She received her first degree from Webber International University in Babson Park, Florida. Moving to the west coast of Florida, she earned an MBA from the University of Tampa. Her education also includes advanced executive training from The University of Pennsylvania's Wharton School of

Business, Bradley University, Disney Institute, and both the American Management Association and the American Marketing Association.

She is a former membership association executive with over two decades of national and international experience, including Vice President of Member Experience with the American Automobile Association (AAA). Velma is a Certified Marketing Executive from Sales & Marketing Executives International; a graduate trainer and coach for Dale Carnegie; and a certified speaker, trainer, and coach for the John Maxwell Team.

A member of Toastmasters International and a Professional Member of the National Speakers Association, Velma is an international keynote speaker who has presented in Australia, Canada, the Bahamas, and across the United States. Her audiences vary from executive boards to elementary students and her expertise includes communication, leadership, team performance, marketing, and membership growth. When she is not helping leaders and organizations discover their value, you can find her enjoying nature, watching birds, and photographing memorable moments. She is currently working on her second book in *the Valuable Leader* series.

Contact Velma:

Email: Velma@LeadersPathway.com

Tel: 941-200-0809

Connect with Velma on social media:

Website: https://LeadersPathway.com

LinkedIn:
https://www.linkedin.com/in/velmaknowles/

Facebook:
https://www.facebook.com/LeadersPathway/

Available Programs: Go Beyond the Book

- Are You *The Valuable Leader:* Seven Steps to Greater Growth, Value, and Influence.

- Do Birds of a Feather Flock Together? Learn the 4 Communication Preferences

- Will The Real Me Please Stand Up? Finding My Personal Brand And Living it Out

- Are You Now The Marketer Too? Learning My A.B.C.'s of Marketing For Growth

- Why Don't You Love Me Like You Used Too? Getting My Members To Renew Again

- How to Grow Your Membership from the Inside Out? Leveraging the Power of Your People, Processes and Promotions

- The Leadership Experience

NOTES

_____

_____

_____

_____

_____

_____

_____

_____

_____

_____

_____

_____

_____

_____

_____

_____

_____

_____

_____

_____

_____

_____

_____

_____

_____

_____

_____

_____

_____

_____

Made in the USA
Lexington, KY
08 October 2018